GASTRIC SLEEVE BARIATRIC COOKBOOK

Tasty and Healthy Recipes for Your New Stomach. Transform Your Eating Habits to Avoid Weight Regain and Embrace Your New Life.

4-Week Recovery Meal Plan Included

By Taste Books

Table of Contents

Introduction

Although your doctor may have given you some dietary suggestions or directed you to a Nutritionist, this guide can assist you in discovering additional recipes. This resource offers proven tips, tactics, and blender recipes for creating flavorful dishes that can assist gastric sleeve patients in their recovery process. Following surgery, you've lost a portion of your stomach and must now create appetizing menu options that can be consumed in small portions for several weeks. Although you will require supplements for the rest of your life, you must ensure that you receive enough nutrients from considerably less food than you are accustomed to eating. After surgery, you may not feel well for a few weeks, and spending time in the kitchen may not be desirable. However, you must consume healthy and delicious meals and drinks. This guide contains techniques that will make it easier for you to navigate this challenging period. You'll also find a variety of recipes for simple, delectable, and nutritious smoothies and shakes, as well as suggestions for soft food combinations to assist you in your journey back to good health. You'll undoubtedly continue to make some of the delectable smoothies and shakes after you've recovered! Following bariatric surgery, the real work toward weight loss begins. The patient will be required to adhere to a strict diet for the body to recover and adjust to the new size of the stomach. This diet requires participants to eat smaller, more frequent meals for the rest of their lives. Of course, because the stomach can only hold small portions of food and the food is quickly depleted, the dieter must eat more frequently. The Gastric Sleeve Diet consists of several phases. It is intended to assist people in preparing for surgery, recovering from surgery, and transitioning to eating healthy meals for the rest of their lives. If you believe the surgery will be too difficult for you, you can try the Gastric Sleeve Surgery Diet. If you want to make lifestyle changes and eat healthier, the Gastric Sleeve diet could be the answer. You can follow the strict eating rules that it provides without undergoing surgery. If you are considering surgery but have not yet made a decision, you can try the diet instead.

Let's dive in.

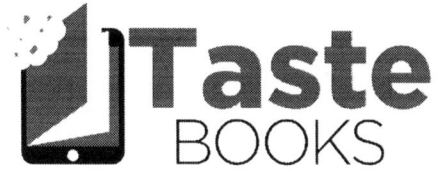

Dear customer,

First of all, we would like to thank you for trusting us by choosing our cookbook.

If you will like our cookbook we would be really happy to see your review on amazon!

If you should encounter problems with any of our recipes, please do not hesitate to contact to us at our email tastebooksus@gmail.com.

Best regards,

Taste Books

REMEMBER TO ALWAYS CONSULT YOUR DOCTOR OR NUTRITIONIST

CHAPTER 1

Chapter 1: What Is Gastric Sleeve Bariatric Surgery?

Gastrectomy is a surgical operation that eliminates a portion of the stomach. Bariatric surgery utilizing a gastric sleeve is a costly procedure that substantially reduces the overall size of the stomach and restricts the amount of food that can be consumed at one time. It does not hinder the absorption of supplements or bypass the digestive organs. After consuming a small quantity of food, you will feel full quickly and for a few hours. Gastric bariatric surgery may also decrease cravings and the amount of "hunger hormone" produced by the stomach, which could aid in weight reduction.

Sleeve gastrectomy, also known as gastric bariatric surgery, has become a popular option for patients seeking significant weight loss through a simple procedure that does not require assistance and long-term complication rates of a lap-band. Individuals with a high BMI (more than 45) are at greater risk during any medical procedure. Additionally, the longer the sedation period, the higher the risk. Gastric bypass surgery can take up to two hours, while duodenal switch surgery frequently lasts more than four hours. This extended sedation period prompted experts to divide the procedure into two stages. The initial goal was to reduce stomach size, while the second phase would occur one year later, after the individual has lost some weight. This final part of the procedure involves bypassing a portion of the digestive tract to decrease calorie absorption. After roughly 75% of the stomach is removed, a tight gastric sleeve or cylinder is formed. Because of these known risk factors, the decision to use a two-phase approach is sometimes made beforehand. During the surgical procedure, the choice to perform sleeve surgery (rather than bypass) is made under certain circumstances. This option is appropriate for patients with an abnormally large liver or extensive scar tissue, which would make the bypass procedure excessively lengthy or risky.

The Benefits of Gastric Sleeve Surgery

Gastric bariatric sleeve surgery is a minimally invasive medical procedure that reduces the size of the stomach. It is now the most commonly used weight loss operation in medical procedures all over the world. Sleeve surgery is thought to be far more effective than gastric band surgery. It does not necessitate the use of an external device or needle modifications, as the latter does. Patients lose a significant amount of weight by engaging in a simple, stress-free activity. It stands to reason that if you have a small stomach, you'll be able to eat less and slim down.

Carrying excessive load puts a lot of strain on your joints, resulting in constant pain and joint damage. The significant and supported weight loss that occurs after bariatric medical procedures reduces the load on joints and frequently allows individuals to discontinue using uncomfortable medications and appreciate significantly more mobility. Achieving and maintaining a healthy weight range frequently allows people with sleep apnea to stop using a cpap machine at night.

Bariatric surgery results in long-term reduction of type 2 diabetes. The outcomes of this strategy are especially promising for obese or overweight patients with type 2 diabetes, allowing nearly all patients to be free of insulin and subordinate prescriptions for three years after the procedure. Many obese people are discouraged because of their helpless self-perception and social shame. Significantly more young people who carry a critical abundance of weight find it difficult to participate in exercises they may enjoy, prompting social isolation and discouragement that leads to depression. Slimming down can improve these patients' enthusiasm.

Weight loss surgery can also improve fertility conditions during childbearing years and reduce a person's risk of coronary disease, stroke, and peripheral coronary disease. Indeed it can help with metabolic disorders, pregnancy complications, gallbladder disease, and other issues. Circulatory strain and cholesterol levels can return to normal or near-normal levels following bariatric surgery, lowering these risks and improving overall health.

The benefits listed above are very encouraging and can be beneficial to those who are involved. With heftiness and its associated health issues spreading at an alarming rate around the world, bariatric surgery unquestionably speaks to be an incredible asset for providing supported alleviation to overweight individuals.

Getting Ready for Gastric Bariatric Surgery

Preparing for any surgery may appear difficult, but it can be done quickly with the help of the following steps, which will give you all the good and positive stuff to get yourself ready.

Begin to think of food as a fundamental fuel for your body, and pay attention to how you react to it. Increase your focus on external cues, just as satiation (a sense of fullness) does. Concentrate on eating slowly, biting thoroughly, tasting thoroughly, and appreciating your food. Instead avoid eating while doing something else, such as working at your desk or watching television. Reduce or eliminate responsive consumption when you are exhausted, drained, stressed, or using food to cope with feelings. It is critical not to gain weight while preparing for the medical procedure. Maintain a strategic distance from your last meal and avoid completely stuffing your stomach. Every day, try to eat three regular meals and one to two small snacks. When planning dinners, remember to include breakfast and try not to eat within four hours of going to bed. Concentrate on increasing protein; incorporate fresh fruits and vegetables into your meal plans, while decreasing or eliminating high fat and sugar nourishments, for example, fast food and other restaurant chains. Recording your eating and drinking habits can reveal valuable information and assist you in identifying opportunities for growth. Make use of various food and fluid trackers.

If you aren't already working out, start gradually and make a consistent physical movement plan that works for you. Short walks, seat exercises, and small increments in everyday activities can all have an effect. Develop practice time little by little by including a few moments of physical activity each day.

Smoking has been shown to significantly increase the risk of complications during and after bariatric surgery. Patients should abstain from tobacco and all nicotine products for at least three months before beginning pre-medical procedure instructions.

Consider which factors have contributed to your weight gain and what has been in the way of making changes throughout your life. Evaluate your readiness for change right now. Think about keeping a diary to help you with the lifestyle improvements you're making. Create a supportive group of people comprised of constructive and caring individuals. Begin by reading various books, visiting various websites, and speaking with other people who have had medical procedures to become educated about the available methods, risks, and changes that will occur in your lifestyle. Always keep in mind that this is a process that takes time. Take small steps, set reasonable goals, and always maintain a positive attitude.

Phases of the Gastric Sleeve Diet

The diet plan for gastric sleeve surgery is segmented into four different stages. This eating regimen is designed to support patients from pre-surgery preparation to post-surgery recovery and long-term lifestyle changes. Its primary goal is to avoid overeating and aid in the success of the procedure. However, to achieve good results with the gastric sleeve diet, you must be fully committed to the process. Each stage of the diet is progressive and it's designed to prevent the stomach from going into shock. Initially, the stomach will be too delicate to accept substantial quantities of food. By slowly increasing the amount of what you eat, you can gradually acclimate your stomach to its new size. The gastric sleeve diet simplifies this process by providing specific guidelines on which foods to consume at each stage. In addition, if you are having gastric sleeve surgery, your surgeon may require you to follow a special pre-operative diet. This is intended to keep you healthy enough for the operation. Before the surgery, you should discuss a pre-operative diet with your surgeon. The diets that each person should follow prior to surgery can vary, so you should get all of the details from your doctor ahead of time.

The First Phase (Week 1)

The first phase of the diet covers the first week following surgery. At this point, you should only bring clear liquids. This is critical because your new stomach requires a lot of hydration to heal. Proper hydration can hasten the healing process and alleviate symptoms such as nausea and vomiting. You might think it's difficult to stick to a liquid diet, but for people who have the surgery, it's relatively easy because they won't be hungry. During phase one, you should only drink clear liquids. Sugary drinks, caffeinated drinks, carbonated drinks, and soda should be avoided. So you don't want to drink tea or coffee. You should substitute sugar-free beverages for these. Maintain your daily water intake of eight glasses. Jelly, clear broth, sugar-free popsicles, and decaffeinated coffee and tea are some examples of clear liquids you can consume during phase one of your diet. This phase of the diet is designed to aid in the healing of your stomach.

The first phase 7 days meal plan

Days	Breakfast	Lunch/Dinner	A.m. Snack/ P.m. Snack
1	Ginger, pineapple juice	Strawberry cucumber thyme-infused water	Beet citrus drink
2	Healthy green juice	Ginger citrus drink	Refreshing carrot drink
3	Beet citrus drink	Ginger citrus drink	Healthy peach drink
4	Ginger, pineapple juice	Beet citrus drink	Refreshing carrot drink
5	Ginger honey lemonade	Strawberry cucumber thyme-infused water	Refreshing carrot drink
6	Old spice ginger tea	Refreshing carrot drink	Strawberry cucumber thyme-infused water
7	Pumpkin ginger latte	Purifying green tea	Ginger pineapple drink

The Second Phase (Week 2)

This phase of the diet begins one week after surgery when the patient becomes hungry. They can start with a protein-rich diet at this point. What you should do is switch to a completely liquid diet that is high in protein. You can achieve this quickly by incorporating sugar-free protein powder into your diet. It's recommended to consume a healthy and nourishing diet while steering clear of sugary foods and other items that provide little to no Nutritional value. Sugary and high-fat foods are among the foods you should avoid during this phase. You should consume up to 20 g of protein per day and drink plenty of water. Thin soups, diluted juice, low-sugar applesauce diluted with water, and other foods are acceptable.

The Second Phase 7 Days Meal Plan

Days	Breakfast	Lunch/Dinner	A.m. Snack/ P.m. Snack
1	Beetroot & parsley smoothie	Creamy milk smoothie	Grapes and peach smoothie
2	Buttery banana shake	Berries almond shake	Melon and nuts smoothie
3	Light fiber smoothie	Meal replacement smoothie with banana	Peach and kiwi smoothie
4	Grapes and peach smoothie	Blue breeze shake	Twin berry smoothie
5	Buttery banana shake	Creamy milk smoothie	White bean smoothie
6	Buttery banana shake	Grapes and peach smoothie	Cashew boost smoothie
7	Cashew boost smoothie	Light fiber smoothie	White bean smoothie

The Third Phase (Week 3)

During the third phase of your diet, it is recommended to consume soft foods that are rich in protein and hydrating. Your diet should consist of 60 g to 80 g of protein and an ample amount of water. It is permissible to consume pureed foods as long as they do not contain any added sugars. However, it is best to avoid foods that are not soft, such as rice, bread, white pasta, high-fat foods, raw vegetables, seeds, and the skin of fruits and vegetables. It is important to prioritize nutrient-dense and high-protein foods to accelerate your recovery after surgery and achieve a feeling of fullness. Foods such as eggs, soups, soft fish, low-fat deli meats, steamed or boiled vegetables, and low-fat cheese are recommended during this phase. Furthermore, continuing your daily protein supplements is essential to meet your protein requirements.

The Third Phase 7 Days Meal Plan

Days	Breakfast	Lunch/Dinner	A.m. Snack/ P.m. Snack
1	Broccoli cauliflower mash	Delicious pureed chicken	Egg white scramble
2	Peanut butter cup smoothies	Cheesy tomato omelet	Delicious pureed chicken
3	Egg white scramble	Broccoli cauliflower mash	Strawberries with whipped yogurt
4	Strawberries with whipped yogurt	Broccoli cauliflower mash	Gazpacho
5	Broccoli cauliflower mash	Delicious pureed chicken	Peanut butter cup smoothies
6	Lemon-blackberry frozen yogurt	Cheesy tomato omelet	Delicious pureed chicken
7	Lemon-blackberry frozen yogurt	Delicious pureed chicken	Gazpacho

The Fourth Phase (Week 4)

This is the stage at which you can finally start eating solid foods. After four weeks from the date of surgery, phase four usually begins. If you are unwilling to have the surgery but would like to follow the diet, you must start at phase four. Phases one through three are designed to help the body adjust to its new stomach size while also supporting the stomach during recovery. If you have not undergone the procedure, you can skip the phases and begin with phase four of the gastric sleeve diet. In phase four, it is important to continue consuming protein shakes and aim for a daily protein intake of 60 to 80 g. Additionally, it is important to stay hydrated throughout the day. However, it is crucial to avoid drinking any liquids within thirty minutes before or after each meal. During this stage, your doctor may also advise you to take a daily bariatric multivitamin. You should limit yourself to three small meals and two small snacks per day. Sugary, low-fiber, and processed foods and snacks should be avoided. This means you should prioritize foods that provide you with the Nutritional value you require. You want to avoid the negative effects that calorie-laden drinks can have. You should also avoid fried foods, sodas, bread, and grains. At this stage, you can safely consume lean meats, low-fat cottage cheese, vegetables, fish, and fruits. Remember that whatever you take will be in small amounts. You want to get used to having a smaller stomach and avoid shocking your stomach with too much food.

The Fourth Phase Meal Plan

Days	Breakfast	Lunch/Dinner	A.m. Snack/ P.m. Snack
1	Light Chicken souvlaki	Ground beef skillet	Feta tomato sea bass
2	Eggs with spinach	Shrimp fra diavolo	Maple-mashed sweet potatoes
3	Mushroom-egg casserole	Simple one-pot mussels	Green tea smoothie
4	Corn meal mush with Polish sausage	Tasty lamb kabobs	Pureed classic egg salad
5	Egg and black beans scramble	Salmon with peas and parsley dressing	Savory cheese biscuits
6	Sweet potato and rosemary waffles	Lemon chicken skewers	Feta tomato sea bass
7	Colorful scrambled eggs	Lamb burgers	Salmon and broccoli

CHAPTER 2
Curing Bariatric Surgery Through Diet

Improving your diet can provide numerous advantages. When undergoing surgery, especially one involving the stomach, a person must be extremely cautious about his or her eating habits. The healthier and simpler the diet, the better the results on the individual's body.

Principles of Nutrition and Gastric Sleeve Bariatric Surgery

Weight loss surgery cannot make you fit; it is only intended to get you started on the path to a healthier physique. It is critical to accept responsibility for your own wellness. After surgery, you must be extremely dedicated and lavish yourself with care and love. Keep a healthy, safe, and positive environment around you. Avoid any unnecessary stress. To achieve better results, you should focus on a completely different way of life after the medical procedure and follow a few simple rules. These are some Nutritional facts and principles that you can easily implement to get your body into the shape you desire.

Avoid sugary foods and beverages, such as sodas, sweets, and alcoholic beverages, and always read the Nutritional label before consuming anything. Eat slowly: chewing your food thoroughly should be your top priority. Try eating your meal in 25 to 30 min, and if necessary, use a stopwatch. Avoid snacking excessively and try to eat three complete meals per day. It is recommended that you drink 60 ounces of fluid per day. It is always recommended to avoid dehydration and constipation after surgery. It is recommended that you consume approximately 60 grams of protein per day following surgery. Foods with a high fat or fiber content are also avoided after surgery because the stomach has to work too hard to digest such substances, which can cause stress in the individual's body. It is also advised to stop eating before reaching satiety after surgery. You should not force yourself to eat anything. It is normal to feel almost no hunger during the initial post-operative period. From the start, you are likely to consume far less food than you require, but this is not a major issue for the time being. It is critical to stay hydrated with low to no calorie fluids and begin utilizing food to teach yourself new habits that will assist you in advancing consistent weight loss. Since food is consumed in such small quantities following surgery, it is advised to take various Nutritional supplements, such as vitamins and minerals.

Smoking and drinking alcoholic beverages are not permitted after surgery. The lining of the stomach walls is extremely sensitive to these substances so they can cause severe irritation. Likewise, it is also advised not to drink while eating. The stomach swells when we drink with food and this condition could harm your stomach walls, which are extremely sensitive right after surgery. Stop drinking at least 30 min before eating.

Remember to return to your doctor after a few days. Routine checkups after surgery are required and always recommended. Take all medications as prescribed by your doctor; nothing should be taken on your own. Any medication can cause ulcers to form after surgery. Consider that it is recommended to do appropriate physical exercise to keep the body from stiffening.

Developing a Weight-Loss Diet That Works After Surgery

It is not difficult to create a diet plan that will help you lose weight after gastric bariatric surgery if you follow the simple guidelines of what to eat and what to avoid after the surgery. Some foods can be difficult to consume after surgery, but they are not completely avoided. Even mentioned earlier, these guidelines must be followed for a diet that will help you lose weight gradually without compromising your body's Nutritional needs.

- Take proper meals that include all food groups. Increase your protein intake in your diet because your body will need to recover from surgery. It is advised to avoid foods with added sugar.

- Avoid using straws when drinking beverages because they introduce air into the stomach, causing discomfort and irritation later on. Drink plenty of water, but eating between meals is strictly forbidden after 30 minutes.

- Avoid foods that are high in fiber, fat, or carbohydrates. Your daily caloric intake should not be more than 1000 calories. Try to consume 300-400 calories at first so your body does not have to do too much work.

- Following surgery, two liters of fluid are advised. You can meet this goal if you drink eight cups of water throughout the day.

- Because your body becomes highly sensitive to alcohol after surgery and absorbs it much faster than before, alcoholic beverages are not permitted.

- It is also advised to eat mindfully, which means that eating while distracted by work or television is not permitted. Healthcare providers recommend taking a one-minute break after each bite.

- Before eating fruits and vegetables, they should be peeled. Avoid using the white membranes found in citrus fruits such as oranges, grapefruit, and lemons, which are actually fibers.

- Consume small amounts of meat. It is advised to chew slowly following surgery. Snacking should be avoided completely after surgery for the best weight loss results. Tough meat is difficult to chew, so try to use tender meat and its products after surgery instead.

- Fruit juices should be diluted in a 50:50 ratio before consumption.

Living a Normal and Healthy Life After Surgery

The vast majority of people believe that the surgery simply causes people to eat less by making their stomachs very small. Nonetheless, researchers have discovered that it causes significant changes in a patient's physiology, altering the movement of thousands of qualities in the human body as well as the complex hormonal motioning from the gut to the brain. It frequently causes perplexing changes in the way things taste, effectively removing the desire for a rich slice of chocolate cake or a sack of burgers. Individuals who undergo the procedure usually lose weight.

Bariatric surgery creates a small stomach pocket. Sleeve gastrectomy reduces the stomach to 25% of its original size; there is also lap band surgery, in which a device is placed around the stomach to prevent eating, and duodenal switch surgery, in which 70% of the stomach is removed, and a large portion of the small digestive system is rerouted. All of these procedures have the same goal, to help seriously obese patients lose weight quickly and effectively by limiting the amount they can eat as well as the number of calories they consume. Bariatric surgery also allows obese patients to control their associated conditions, such as diabetes, hypertension, and sleep apnea. Tumors are linked to obesity, particularly colon, bosom, and endometrial cancers. We don't have long-term studies to show that people who have been overweight for a long time and then have weight loss surgery have a lower chance. In any case, we believe that working ahead of time (and keeping people less fatty for a long time) will reduce these cancer risks. Bariatric surgery patients also have fewer hospitalizations, shorter emergency clinic stays, and are less likely to be admitted to the intensive care unit. This is in contrast to obese patients who do not have a bariatric procedure. According to studies, more bariatric patients are alive than individuals who did not have a procedure. We've also seen improvements in women with polycystic ovary disease, barrenness, ulcers, and leg growth. We discover health benefits whenever we pivot. It's a risk that some patients are willing to take. The more exhausted you are as a result of your weight, the greater the benefit of having the procedure. A bariatric procedure will help you achieve your life goals.

How to Reduce Excess Skin

One common issue that patients may experience after gastric sleeve surgery is excess skin. As the body adjusts to the new weight and shape, the skin may not be able to keep up, resulting in loose or sagging skin. Various methods can be used to help reduce excess skin, including both surgical and non-surgical treatments.

In this part, we will explore natural methods for reducing excess skin after gastric sleeve surgery. These methods can complement other treatments and help patients achieve their desired results in a safe and holistic manner.

Hydration

One of the simplest but most effective ways to reduce excess skin after gastric sleeve surgery is by staying hydrated. When the body is dehydrated, the skin may appear dull and lack elasticity, which can exacerbate excess skin. Drinking plenty of water can help keep the skin hydrated and improve its appearance.

In addition to drinking water, patients can also include water-rich foods in their diet to help increase hydration levels. Fruits and vegetables such as watermelon, cucumber, and lettuce are great options.

Exercise

Regular exercise can help improve muscle tone and skin elasticity, which can reduce the appearance of excess skin. Exercise can also help patients maintain their weight loss and improve their overall health.

Patients should aim for a combination of strength training and cardiovascular exercise to achieve the best results. Strength training can help build muscle, which can fill out loose skin and improve its appearance. Cardiovascular exercise can help burn fat and improve circulation, which can help improve skin health.

Diet

A healthy diet rich in nutrients can also help improve skin health and reduce the appearance of excess skin after gastric sleeve surgery. Patients should aim to consume a balanced diet that includes plenty of fruits, vegetables, lean protein, and healthy fats.

Foods rich in collagen can also be beneficial for skin health. Collagen is a protein that helps maintain skin elasticity and reduce wrinkles. Foods such as bone broth, fish, and nuts are all great sources of collagen.

Skincare

Taking care of the skin can also help reduce the appearance of excess skin after gastric sleeve surgery. Patients should aim to keep their skin moisturized and protect it from the sun. Using a good quality moisturizer can help improve skin elasticity and reduce dryness.

In addition, patients should also consider using products that contain retinoids, which can help reduce the appearance of wrinkles and improve skin texture. Retinoids can be found in various skincare products, including creams and serums.

Reducing excess skin after gastric sleeve surgery can be a challenging process, but natural methods can be effective when used in combination with other treatments. Patients should aim to stay hydrated, exercise regularly, consume a healthy diet, and take care of their skin. By making these lifestyle changes, patients can achieve their desired results and improve their overall health and well-being.

How to Prevent Hair Loss Due to Surgery?

Hair loss prevention after surgery does not need fancy deeds to be carried out successfully. Instead, it will only need simple yet valuable steps which you can incorporate into your daily life and activities.

Good Hair Care Tips for Preventing Hair Loss

The following tips will help you prevent hair loss:

- Eat a well-balanced diet especially foods that are rich in vitamins such as A, B, C and E, iron, and protein.

- Comb or brush your hair gently and try to use wide-toothed combs as much as possible.

- Use mild and gentle shampoos for washing your hair.

- Avoid applying extreme heat to your hair such as with hair straighteners and hair dryers since these products may tend to damage the hair and make it brittle.

- Try to avoid stress as much as possible as this could contribute to the occurrence of certain types of hair loss, not to mention how it could cause adverse effects on your overall health.

- Massage your scalp with essential oil every once in a while.

- Drink plenty of water.

- Quit smoking.

- Make sure your body gets enough exercise.

- Avoid combing your hair while it is still wet.

- Avoid applying hair products with too much chemicals in them.

- Avoid wearing your hair in very tight hairstyles which can cause hair breakage and which will eventually lead to hair loss.

- Keep your hair and scalp clean as much as possible.

Foods that Help Prevent Hair Loss

Some of the healthy foods which can significantly help in preventing hair loss include the following.

Beans – Beans are a very rich source of vitamins B, vitamin C, protein and other essential minerals which are greatly beneficial for optimum hair growth. It also contains a good amount of iron which is another essential nutrient for preventing hair loss.

Salmon – This particular type of fatty fish is indeed a gem when it comes to preventing hair loss. Aside from containing a rich amount of protein and B vitamins, salmon is also considered to be a very rich source of omega-3 fatty acids which play a very essential role in promoting good hair growth.

Eggs – This very simple food is not as simple as it may seem when it comes to the nutrients it carries. Eggs are a very great source of protein and other minerals such as sulfur. It is also loaded with iron which is very beneficial for carrying oxygen to the hair follicles.

These are just some of the wide variety of foods that can help you prevent hair loss. Including healthy foods like these in your diet is a very simple but at the same time a great favor that you can do to your body. Treat your body well and your body will thank you in return.

Using Spices

Various spices can help you with your baldness. These are generally applied on the impacted scalp. Depending on your balding condition, the impact of each spice is unique.

Cassia Auriculata is one of the essential fixings in many hair products. It invigorates hair growth by expanding the flow of blood to the scalp. It also works as an antibacterial and a toner that treats scalp problems. This advances shiny and voluminous hair.

Hibiscus Rosa-Sinensis is known as China rose. It has been known to animate hair development. As a therapeutic flower, it prevents hair loss and premature graying. It also helps treat scalp problems.

Henna or Mehndi is known to variety, purge, and condition the hair. It has been utilized for a long time by royals as it likewise gives a glossy completion.

The mehndi calms the scalp, diminishes hair fall, and adds volume to the hair.

Curry leaves might be more known to add flavor to food; however, it is likewise a great treatment for hair. It revives the hair and fortifies hair follicles. It likewise advances hair development as it goes about as an enemy of oxidants.

Chrysopogon zizanioides is a spice that invigorates the circulatory framework furthermore, supports the hair shaft.

The flower petals are used to soothe and nourish the hair. It eliminates flaky skin and increments blood stream which lessens hair fall and adds hair volume.

Neem is used to treat baldness as it stimulates hair growth. It has fatty acids that strengthen hair and has been used for thousands of years.

Taking Supplements

Taking enhancements is an elective answer for finishing the supplements you need. Nonetheless, don't take these without a specialist's solution. Request a counselor.

Counseling a specialist can assist with saving you from additional inconvenient circumstances. Some enhancements may not be for you, particularly on the off chance that you have other wellbeing concerns.

Dealing with your general well-being can improve hair. Thinning hair can be a difficult problem for some, especially women and children. It can cause pressure close to home, which could reduce self-confidence. Plan for it now so you don't have to deal with it later. If you already have this, remember that there are certain strategies to help you adjust to it. Take a look at these to see which one is best for you. See a specialist to help you also make sure you're taking the right medication, and indeed even help you manage your eating regimen.

Protein is important in advancing hair development. It helps to invigorate you, which is why it's recommended to eat a few servings, around three ounces, of meat, dairy, and beans every day.

Food sources rich in omega-3 are also important for the diet. This can be tracked down in nuts, seeds, and fish. This reduces irritation and improves the scalp.

Iron is also prescribed to reduce the risk of weakness, which is one of the main drivers of baldness. It also promotes better blood flow which promotes hair growth.

L-ascorbic acid improves iron ingestion. These are found in food sources, for example, oranges, strawberries and grapes.

Zinc and biotin advances hair development, particularly for individuals with metabolic problems.

In addition to going for baldness therapy during an operation or home treatment for your baldness, be sure to also incorporate a good diet. Take a look at your food intake and also make sure you set a decent menu. Familiarize yourself with the right foods that provide you with the nutrients you need for better hair.

Shopping List

- Apples
- Asparagus
- Bananas
- Bell peppers
- Berries
- Broccoli
- Cabbage
- Carrots
- Cauliflower
- Celery
- Green beans
- Kiwis
- Lemons/limes
- Lettuce
- Mango
- Melons
- Cherries
- Cucumbers
- Eggplant/squash
- Grapefruit
- Grapes
- Mushrooms
- Onions
- Oranges
- Peaches
- Pears
- Peas
- Potatoes (sweet/white)
- Tomatoes
- Zucchini
- Any fresh fish (salmon, tuna, mackerel, trout, catfish, roughy, tilapia
- Any shellfish (oysters, clams, shrimp)
- Skinless Poultry (turkey/chicken, ground chicken/turkey, or breast)
- Lean deli or lean pre-packaged lunch meats
- Lean beef (round, cubed steak, London broil, flank steak, 96% lean ground beef
- Lean pork (tenderloin, loin chops, Canadian bacon)
- Wild game (venison, quail, etc.)
- Unsweetened or light soy milk
- Greek yogurt
- Low-fat or light yogurt

Foods to Avoid

- Fast food
- Sugary snacks
- Bread
- Cooking oils
- Desserts
- Carbonated drinks
- Caffeinated drinks (tea and coffee, for example)
- Sugary drinks
- Alcohol

Tips for Eating Out

- Do your research ahead of time.

- Bring your special menu request card with you.

- Choose appropriate portion sizes.

- Practice mindfulness.

- Separate food and fluids.

- Limit your consumption of carbonated beverages and empty calories.

CHAPTER 3

Phase1 Clear Fluids Recipes

1. Beet Citrus Drink

Preparation Time: 10 minutes   *Cooking Time: 0 minutes*   *Servings: 2*

Ingredients:
- 2 beets
- 1 tangerine
- 1 orange
- 1 lime
- 2 carrots
- 2 cups dandelion greens
- 2-inch knob ginger

Directions:
1. Add all ingredients to the juicer and juice. Enjoy!

Nutrition Facts (per serving):
Calories: 229 kcal, Fats: 1.7 g, Carbs: 45.2 g, Proteins: 8.2 g

2. Ginger Citrus Drink

Preparation Time: 10 minutes   *Cooking Time: 0 minutes*   *Servings: 1*

Ingredients:
- 1 lemon, peeled
- 1-inch knob fresh ginger root, finely grated
- 1 orange, peeled
- 1 grapefruit, peeled
- A pinch cayenne pepper

Directions:
1. Juice all the ingredients in a juicer, except cayenne pepper; stir in cayenne pepper and serve.

Nutrition Facts (per serving):
Calories: 159 kcal, Fats: 0.5 g, Carbs: 35.2 g, Proteins: 3.5 g

3. Ginger Honey Lemonade

⅜ Preparation Time: 2 minutes　　　　*☺ Cooking Time: 0 minutes*　　　　*☞ Servings: 1*

🥣 Ingredients:
- Lemon slices for garnish, if desired
- 1 medium sprig of fresh rosemary
- Ice cubes
- 1/6 cup honey
- ½ large sprig of fresh rosemary for garnish, if desired
- 2 large strips lemon peel
- 1 tbsp fresh ginger root, grated
- 2 lemons juice
- Water

🗷 Directions:
1. Combine together sprigs of fresh rosemary, lemon peel, ginger, and honey, and add 1 cup of water in a small pot.
2. Bring the mixture to a boil, then simmer on low heat for about 10 minutes, stirring frequently.
3. Let cool for about 15 minutes, then strain the mixture into a large pitcher. Discard the rosemary and ginger.
4. Add the lemon juice and 3 cups of cold water to the pitcher, then combine.
5. To serve, pour over ice along with a lemon slice and a little piece of fresh rosemary as a garnish, if desired.

Nutrition Facts (per serving):
Calories: 129 kcal, Fats: 0.5 g, Carbs: 29.6 g, Proteins: 2.1 g

4. Ginger Pineapple Drink

⅜ Preparation Time: 10 minutes　　　　*☺ Cooking Time: 0 minutes*　　　　*☞ Servings: 2*

🥣 Ingredients:
- 1 pineapple center
- 1-inch ginger root
- 2 carrots
- 3 celery stalks
- Handful mint leaves
- A small handful cilantro

🗷 Directions:
1. Juice all the ingredients in a juicer and serve.

Nutrition Facts (per serving):
Calories: 192 kcal, Fats: 1.1 g, Carbs: 40.7 g, Proteins: 5.3 g

5. Ginger, Pineapple Juice

Preparation Time: 10 minutes   *Cooking Time: 0 minutes*   *Servings: 1*

Ingredients:

- ¼ medium pineapple
- 1 lemon, peeled
- 1-inch fresh ginger
- 2 large cucumbers
- 1 cup chopped cabbage
- ½ cup fresh mint

Directions:

1. Juice all the ingredients, one at a time, in a juicer and serve.

Nutrition Facts (per serving):
Calories: 202 kcal, Fats: 2.4 g, Carbs: 36.9 g, Proteins: 7.9 g

6. Healthy Green Juice

Preparation Time: 10 minutes   *Cooking Time: 0 minutes*   *Servings: 2*

Ingredients:

- 2 ½ cups fresh spinach
- 2 large celery stalks
- 2 large green apples, cored and sliced
- 1 medium orange, peeled, seeded, and sectioned
- 1 tbsp fresh lime juice
- 1 tbsp fresh lemon juice

Directions:

1. In a juicer, add all ingredients and extract the juice according to the manufacturer's directions.
2. Transfer into 2 serving glasses and stir in lime and lemon juices.
3. Serve immediately.

Nutrition Facts (per serving):
Calories: 125 kcal, Fats: 0.8 g, Carbs: 26.3 g, Proteins: 3.1 g

7. Healthy Peach Drink

Preparation Time: 5 minutes   *Cooking Time: 5 minutes*   *Servings: 3*

Ingredients:
- 2 fresh lemons juice
- Ice cubes
- 10 tbsp sweetener of choice
- 5 cups water
- 8 peeled peaches, cut into slices

For the Garnish:
- Mint leaves
- Peach slices

Directions:
1. Add peach slices, sweetener of choice, lemon juice, ice cubes, and water in the bowl of your blender and blend on medium speed. Blend another time until smooth.
2. Pour the drink over ice in a glass and garnish with mint leaves and peach slices, if desired.

Nutrition Facts (per serving):
Calories: 124 kcal, Fats: 0.6 g, Carbs: 26.2 g, Proteins: 3.7 g

8. Old Spice Ginger Tea

Preparation Time: 10 minutes   *Cooking Time: 0 minutes*   *Servings: 2*

Ingredients:
- 8 cups water
- 1 (4-inch) piece fresh ginger, chopped
- 4 lemons, sliced
- 6 cardamom pods, bruised
- 1 cinnamon stick
- 1 whole star anise pod
- 3 tbsp organic honey

Directions:
1. In a pan, add water over medium-high heat and bring to a boil.
2. Add ginger, lemon slices, and spices, then stir to combine.
3. Reduce the heat to medium-low and simmer for about 5-10 minutes
4. Throw the tea into a pitcher through a strainer, discarding the solids.
5. Stir in honey and serve.

Nutrition Facts (per serving):
Calories: 122 kcal, Fats: 0.4 g, Carbs: 27.7 g, Proteins: 1.9 g

9. Pumpkin Ginger Latte

⅌ Preparation Time: 10 minutes   *🍲 Cooking Time: 0 minutes*   *☕ Servings: 1*

⚗ Ingredients:

- 6 cups water
- ½ lemon, seeded and chopped roughly
- 1 (1-inch) piece fresh ginger, chopped
- 2 tbsp maple syrup
- ⅛ tsp ground turmeric
- Pinch ground cinnamon

▣ Directions:

1. In a pan, add all ingredients over medium-high heat and bring to a boil.
2. Reduce the heat to medium-low and simmer for about 10-12 minutes
3. Strain into a mug and serve hot.

Nutrition Facts (per serving):
Calories: 160 kcal, Fats: 0.6 g, Carbs: 38.3 g, Proteins: 1.4 g

10. Purifying Green Tea

⅌ Preparation Time: 5 minutes   *🍲 Cooking Time: 0 minutes*   *☕ Servings: 4*

⚗ Ingredients:

- 2 cups fresh baby spinach
- 3 cups frozen green grapes
- 1 medium ripe avocado peeled, pitted, and chopped
- 2 tsp organic honey
- 1 ½ cup strong brewed green tea

▣ Directions:

1. In a high-speed blender, add all ingredients and pulse until smooth.
2. Transfer into serving glasses and serve immediately.

Nutrition Facts (per serving):
Calories: 236 kcal, Fats: 13.5 g, Carbs: 20 g, Proteins: 3 g

11. Refreshing Carrot Drink

Preparation Time: 10 minutes   *Cooking Time: 0 minutes*   *Servings: 2*

Ingredients:

- 4 carrots
- 1 cup sprouts
- 1-cm fresh ginger
- 1 kiwi fruit
- 1 lemon
- 1 green apple
- 1 cucumber
- 2 stalks celery
- 1 cup parsley

Directions:

1. Add all ingredients to the juicer and juice. Enjoy!

Nutrition Facts (per serving):
Calories: 198 kcal, Fats: 2 g, Carbs: 36.4 g, Proteins: 8.7 g

12. Strawberry Cucumber Thyme-Infused Water

Preparation Time: 7 minutes   *Cooking Time: 0 minutes*   *Servings: 1*

Ingredients:

- ½ cup fresh strawberries, sliced
- 4 cups water
- 1 cucumber, sliced
- 5 sprigs thyme

Directions:

1. Add thyme, cucumber, and strawberries in a glass jar.
2. Pour water into the jar and stir well.
3. Place jar in the refrigerator for 1 hour.
4. Serve and enjoy.

Nutrition Facts (per serving):
Calories: 96 kcal, Fats: 2.6 g, Carbs: 14.9 g, Proteins: 3.5 g

CHAPTER 4

Phase 2 Full Liquids Recipes

13. Beetroot & Parsley Smoothie

Preparation Time: 10 minutes   *Cooking Time: 0 minutes*   *Servings: 1*

Ingredients:
- 1 ½ cup carrot
- 1 cup beetroot
- 1 tbsp parsley
- 3 tsp celery
- 1 cup ice

Directions:
1. In a blender, place all ingredients and blend until smooth
2. Pour the smoothie into a glass and serve

Nutrition Facts (per serving):
Calories: 91 kcal, Fats: 0.1 g, Carbs: 17.6 g, Proteins: 4.7 g

14. Berries Almond Shake

Preparation Time: 10 minutes   *Cooking Time: 0 minutes*   *Servings: 1*

Ingredients:
- ½ cup frozen blackberries
- ½ cup frozen strawberries
- ½ cup frozen blueberries
- 3 Medjool dates, pitted and chopped
- 1 cup unsweetened almond milk

Directions:
1. In a high-speed blender, add all ingredients and pulse until smooth.
2. Transfer into serving glasses and serve immediately.

Nutrition Facts (per serving):
Calories: 190 kcal, Fats: 3.9 g, Carbs: 35.1 g, Proteins: 4g

15. Blue Breeze shake

Preparation Time: 10 minutes   *Cooking Time: 0 minutes*   *Servings: 1*

Ingredients:
- ½ cup blueberries
- 1 small banana
- 1 cup chilled unsweetened vanilla almond milk
- Water as needed
- 1 scoop unflavored protein powder

Directions:
1. Mix in a blender for 40-50 seconds and serve as ready.

Nutrition Facts (per serving):
Calories: 174 kcal, Fats: 3.9 g, Carbs: 29.4 g, Proteins: 8.3 g

16. Buttery Banana Shake

Preparation Time: 10 minutes   *Cooking Time: 0 minutes*   *Servings: 2*

Ingredients:
- 1 tbsp raw peanut butter
- 1 cup almond milk
- 1 scoop protein powder, any flavor
- ¼ cup Greek yogurt
- 2 tsp basil
- 2 tsp ginger paste
- 1 tsp vanilla extract
- 1 tsp sesame seeds

Directions:
1. Mix and blend all ingredients in a blender and shake for a whole minute; drink a smooth shake in the morning or evening during workouts.

Nutrition Facts (per serving):
Calories: 154 kcal, Fats: 11.4 g, Carbs: 6.3 g, Proteins: 7.9 g

17. Cashew Boost Smoothie

Preparation Time: 8 minutes   *Cooking Time: 0 minutes*   *Servings: 4*

Ingredients:
- 3 or 4 cups raw cashews
- 1 cup chilled almond milk
- ¼ cup mixed fruit

Directions:
1. Blend all ingredients mixed and serve.

Nutrition Facts (per serving):
Calories: 132 kcal, Fats: 8.7 g, Carbs: 9.7 g, Proteins: 3.8 g

18. Coconut Breezy Shake Dose

Preparation Time: 5 minutes *Cooking Time: 0 minutes* *Servings: 4*

Ingredients:
- 1 cup skimmed milk (chilled)
- 4 tbsp shredded coconut
- Water as needed
- 1 cup pineapple chunks
- ½ scoop of vanilla protein powder

Directions:
1. Mix all the ingredients in a mixer and shake well for 20 seconds; serve when the smooth texture is seen. Pour in a large glass, and use water to make proper smoothness only.

Nutrition Facts (per serving):
Calories: 171 kcal, Fats: 13 g, Carbs: 10 g, Proteins: 6.6 g

19. Coconut Cherry Smoothie

Preparation Time: 8 minutes *Cooking Time: 0 minutes* *Servings: 4*

Ingredients:
- 1 cup nondairy coconut milk
- 4 Ice cubes as needed
- 1 cup mixed berries (blueberries, blackberries, and cherries)
- ½ plantains
- A handful of mixed chopped fruits- pear/peach/guava
- 2 tbsp plain soy yogurt

Directions:
1. Toss in the berries, milk, and other ingredients in a blender, then shake well to make a smooth drink.

Nutrition Facts (per serving):
Calories: 179 kcal, Fats: 12.3 g, Carbs: 14.3 g, Proteins: 2.4 g

20. Creamy Milk Smoothie

Preparation Time: 8 minutes   *Cooking Time: 0 minutes*   *Servings: 1*

Ingredients:
- 1 tsp cinnamon powder
- 1 cup almond milk
- ¼ cup plain soy yogurt
- 1 tsp ground ginger
- 1 tbsp whey protein vanilla
- Spearmint to toss in

Directions:
1. Shake this creamy smoothie with a blending machine and pour it into a glass to drink.

Nutrition Facts (per serving):
Calories: 96 kcal, Fats: 4.3 g, Carbs: 11.5 g, Proteins: 3.6 g

21. Grapes and Peach Smoothie

Preparation Time: 10 minutes   *Cooking Time: 0 minutes*   *Servings: 4*

Ingredients:
- 1 cup red grapes juice
- 3 tbsp shredded coconut
- ½ scoop protein powder
- A handful of chopped pistachios
- 1 small guava and peach chopped
- Ice as required

Directions:
1. Use natural juice to add to the smoothie, mix all the foods in a blender and shake to make it a smooth drink.

Nutrition Facts (per serving):
Calories: 150 kcal, Carbs: 6 g, Proteins: 8 g, Fats: 3 g

22. Light Fiber Smoothie

Preparation Time: 10 minutes   *Cooking Time: 0 minutes*   *Servings: 2*

Ingredients:
- 2 tsp nutmeg
- 1 ½ scoop vanilla protein powder mix
- 1 ½ cup soy milk
- ½ cup low-fat egg nog
- A pinch cinnamon
- 4-5 crushed ice cubes
- 1 lemon zest

Directions:
1. Grab the ingredients, measure them, and add them all in a blender to mix.

Nutrition Facts (per serving):
Calories: 267 kcal, Fats: 9.1 g, Carbs: 39.9 g, Proteins: 6.1 g

23. Meal Replacement Smoothie With Banana

Preparation Time: 10 minutes   *Cooking Time: 0 minutes*   *Servings: 4*

Ingredients:
- 1 large banana (ripped or green)
- 1 cup coconut milk
- A drop vanilla extract
- 1 tbsp natural peanut powder
- 1 tsp carob powder
- Ice as needed
- 4 small fresh berries without stems

Directions:
1. Mix all foods and condiments in milk and shake them all well in an electric machine.

Nutrition Facts (per serving):
Calories: 167 kcal, Fats: 13.5 g, Carbs: 8.6 g, Proteins: 3.1 g

24. Melon and Nuts Smoothie

Preparation Time: 10 minutes   *Cooking Time: 0 minutes*   *Servings: 2*

Ingredients:
- 1 cup watermelon chunks
- ¼ cup mixed nuts
- 1 cup soy milk
- ½ cup tofu
- Chilled water as needed
- 1 scoop of chocolate whey protein powder

Directions:
1. Blend all ingredients greatly to attain a smooth and soft drink.

Nutrition Facts (per serving):
Calories: 169 kcal, Fats: 11.6 g, Carbs: 7.1 g, Proteins: 9.1 g

25. Peach and Kiwi Smoothie

Preparation Time: 8 minutes   *Cooking Time: 0 minutes*   *Servings: 1*

Ingredients:
- 1 cup plain low-fat yogurt
- ½ cup peach chunks
- 1 tbsp protein powder
- Water as needed
- ½ cup kiwi fruit

Directions:
1. Blend powder and fruits finely in liquid, then serve chilled when smooth.

Nutrition Facts (per serving):
Calories: 171 kcal, Fats: 0.9 g, Carbs: 30.7 g, Proteins: 10 g

26. Twin Berry Smoothie

Preparation Time: 10 minutes   *Cooking Time: 0 minutes*   *Servings: 1*

Ingredients:
- ½ cup peach chunks
- ¾ cup almond milk
- A handful cranberries and raspberries
- An orange peel
- 1 scoop protein powder (whey)
- Ice cubes as required

Directions:
1. Chop the berries well, use natural orange peel, add all foods in a blender, then shake to serve.

Nutrition Facts (per serving):
Calories: 136 kcal, Fats: 3.2 g, Carbs: 19.4 g, Proteins: 10 g

27. White Bean Smoothie

Ingredients:
- 1 cup unsweetened rice milk (chilled)
- ¼ cup peach slices
- ¼ cup white beans cooked
- A pinch cinnamon powder
- A pinch nutmeg

Directions:
1. Pour milk into the blender and add the other ingredients to blend till smooth enough to serve and drink.

Nutrition Facts (per serving):
Calories: 80 kcal, Fats: 2.4 g, Carbs: 10.6 g, Proteins: 4.8 g

CHAPTER 5

Phase 3 Soft Foods Recipes

28. Broccoli Cauliflower Mash

Preparation Time: 10 minutes   *Cooking Time: 15 minutes*   *Servings: 2*

Ingredients:
- 4 cups broccoli florets
- 4 cups cauliflower florets
- ¼ tsp onion powder
- 2 cups vegetable stock
- ¼ tsp garlic powder
- 2 tbsp fresh parsley
- 1 tsp sea salt

Directions:
1. Add broccoli and cauliflower florets in a steamer and cook for 15 minutes.
2. Transfer cauliflower, broccoli, stock, garlic powder, onion powder, and parsley to a blender and blend until smooth.
3. Season with salt and serve.

Nutrition Facts (per serving):
Calories: 125 kcal, Fat: 2.1 g, Carbs: 12.7 g, Proteins: 14 g

29. Cheesy Tomato Omelet

Preparation Time: 2 minutes   *Cooking Time: 8 minutes*   *Servings: 2*

Ingredients:
- ½ tsp butter
- 1 large egg
- 1 tbsp milk or water
- Salt
- Black pepper
- Garlic powder
- 1 slice Cheddar cheese
- 1 tbsp tomato, chopped

Directions:
1. In a 6-inch nonstick skillet, melt butter over medium heat; turn the skillet to coat evenly.
2. In a small bowl, whisk egg and milk or water; pour into skillet. Sprinkle garlic powder, pepper, and salt over the top of the egg.
3. When the edges of the egg mixture begin to cook, lift the edges with a spatula and tip the skillet so the uncooked egg flows underneath to cook.
4. Repeat step 3 until the top is almost dry. Place cheese slice on top, then the tomatoes over half of the omelet.
5. When the cheese begins to melt, fold it in half and serve.

Nutrition Facts (per serving):
Calories: 113 kcal, Fats: 9 g, Carbs: 0.8 g, Protein: 7.1 g

30. Delicious Pureed Chicken

Preparation Time: 10 minutes   *Cooking Time: 5 minutes*   *Servings: 2*

Ingredients:

- 1 chicken breast, skinless, boneless, and cooked
- ⅛ tsp onion powder
- 2 tbsp light mayonnaise
- 2 tbsp low-fat yogurt
- Pepper
- Salt

Directions:

1. Add chicken breast into the food processor and process until getting a fine consistency.
2. Add the remaining ingredients and stir everything well.
3. Serve and enjoy.

Nutrition Facts (per serving):
Calories: 180 kcal, Fats: 11.3 g, Carbs: 1.1 g, Proteins: 18.9 g

31. Egg White Scramble

Preparation Time: 5 minutes   *Cooking Time: 5 minutes*   *Servings: 1*

Ingredients:

- ¼ cup non-fat cottage cheese
- 2 egg whites, lightly beaten
- Nonstick cooking spray
- Pinch herbs, dried, such as oregano or basil
- Salt and black pepper, freshly ground, to taste

Directions:

1. In a medium bowl, mash cottage cheese with a fork to break up curds. Add egg whites and beat until smooth.
2. Spray a small nonstick skillet with cooking spray and heat over medium heat. Add the egg mixture, sprinkle with herbs, and stir gently until cooked through 4 to 5 minutes.
3. Mash the cooked egg mixture with a fork to the desired consistency, season to taste with salt and pepper, and serve immediately. Enjoy!

Nutrition Facts (per serving):
Calories: 165 kcal: Fats: 5.3 g: Proteins: 15 g; Carbs: 3.3 g

32. Gazpacho

Preparation Time: 15 minutes + 2 hours refrigerating   Cooking Time: 0 minutes   Servings: 2

Ingredients:

- 1 tbsp vegetable oil
- 1 red bell pepper, diced
- 1 onion, diced
- 2 garlic cloves, minced
- 2 large fresh ripe tomatoes, peeled, diced
- 1 small cucumber, peeled and diced
- 1 tsp lime juice
- 2 tbsp balsamic vinegar
- 1 tbsp fresh basil leaves, chopped
- 1 tsp Kosher salt, plus more to taste
- ½ tsp cumin, ground
- Black pepper, freshly ground, to taste

Directions:

1. In a medium saucepan, heat oil over medium heat and sauté bell pepper and onion until softened, about 5 minutes, stirring occasionally. Add garlic and sauté for about 1 minute more, stirring constantly.
2. Remove the pan from heat and stir in tomatoes, cucumber, lime juice, vinegar, basil, salt, and cumin, and season to taste with pepper.
3. If desired, pour the mixture into a blender container, pulse to desired consistency, or use an immersion blender.
4. Refrigerate the soup until chilled through, about 2 hours. Serve and enjoy!

Nutrition Facts (per serving):
Calories: 245 kcal, Fats: 16.3 g, Proteins: 4.5 g, Carbs: 20 g

33. Lemon-Blackberry Frozen Yogurt

Preparation Time: 10 minutes   Cooking Time: 0 minutes   Servings: 2

Ingredients:

- 4 cups blackberries, frozen
- ½ cup low-fat plain Greek yogurt
- 1 lemon, juiced
- 2 tsp liquid stevia
- Fresh mint leaves, for garnish

Directions:

1. Take your food processor and add blackberries, yogurt, lemon juice, and stevia, blending well until smooth.
2. Serve immediately and enjoy with a garnish of fresh mint leaves.

Nutrition Facts (per serving):
Calories: 108 kcal, Fats: 0.1 g, Proteins: 7.3 g, Carbs: 19.4 g

34. Peanut Butter Cup Smoothies

Preparation Time: 10 minutes   *Cooking Time: 0 minutes*   *Servings: 2*

Ingredients:

- ½ cup skim milk
- ½ cup plain Greek yogurt
- 2 tbsp creamy natural peanut butter
- 1 tbsp unsweetened cocoa powder, sifted
- 8 to 10 ice cubes

Directions:

1. Place all ingredients in a blender container and pulse until thoroughly blended and smooth.
2. Pour into 2 large glasses to serve. Enjoy!

Nutrition Facts (per serving):
Calories: 218 kcal; Fats: 19.2 g: Proteins: 6.4 g: Carbs: 4.3 g

35. Strawberries With Whipped Yogurt

Preparation Time: 10 minutes   *Cooking Time: 0 minutes*   *Servings: 2*

Ingredients:

- 1 cup strawberries, sliced
- 1 cup (8 oz) plain Greek yogurt
- 1 tbsp heavy cream

Directions:

1. Pulse the strawberries in a food processor or blender until mashed or puréed to desired consistency and set aside.
2. In a medium bowl with tall sides, beat yogurt and cream with an electric hand mixer until thickened and stiff peaks form, about 5 minutes.
3. Spoon the strawberries into 2 bowls, top with whipped yogurt, and serve immediately. Enjoy!

Nutrition Facts (per serving):
Calories: 169 kcal, Fats: 12.9 g, Proteins: 7.3 g, Carbs: 6.1 g

CHAPTER 6

Breakfast Recipes

36. Baked Curried Apple Oatmeal Cups

Preparation Time: 10 minutes   *Cooking Time: 20 minutes*   *Servings: 6*

Ingredients:

- 3 ½ cups old-fashioned oats
- 3 tbsp brown sugar
- 2 tsp of your preferred curry powder
- ⅛ tsp salt
- 1 cup unsweetened almond milk
- 1 cup unsweetened applesauce
- 1 tsp vanilla
- ½ cup chopped walnuts

Directions:

1. Preheat the oven to 375°F. Then spray a 12-cup muffin tin with baking spray then set aside.
2. Mix the oats, brown sugar, curry powder, and salt in a medium bowl.
3. Mix the milk, applesauce, and vanilla in a small bowl,
4. Stir the liquid ingredients into the dry ingredients and mix until just combined. Stir in the walnuts.
5. Divide the mixture among the muffin cup using a scant ⅓ cup for each.
6. Bake this for 18 to 20 minutes until the oatmeal is firm. Serve.

Nutrition Facts (per serving):
Calories: 200 kcal, Fats: 8.3 g, Carbs: 25.5 g, Proteins: 5.2 g

Preparation Time: 20 minutes   *Cooking Time: 30 minutes*   *Servings: 1*

Ingredients:

For the Scrambled Egg:

- ⅛ tsp salt
- 1 egg
- ⅛ tsp pepper

For the Black Beans Puree:

- 3 tbsp bbq sauce
- ½ cup rinsed black beans
- 2 tbsp vegetable or chicken broth
- 1 tbsp protein powder

Directions:

For the black beans puree:

1. Put the beans in a small-sized saucepan on medium heat. Then add the enchilada sauce. Heat for 2 min, stirring all the time. Then add the chicken broth. Mix well.
2. Add the mixture to a blender or use one hand blender to make a smooth mixture. Transfer it into one bowl.
3. Let it cool a bit, and then mix in the protein powder. Stir well. Cover it to keep it warm till you cook the egg.
4. Keep the leftovers in the fridge so that you can eat them at some other time.

For the scrambled eggs:

1. Heat a small nonstick pan on medium heat. Break the egg in a small bowl and whisk it well to incorporate air into it.
2. Pour the egg into the heated pan. Sprinkle with pepper and salt. Use a rubber spatula to stir the egg in the pan while it cooks. When it is almost done and still has a slightly liquid texture, fold it and put it on a plate.
3. Spread over one tablespoon of the black beans puree and one teaspoon of bbq sauce over the eggs.

Nutrition Facts (per serving):

Calories: 207 kcal, Fats: 6 g, Carbs: 21.4 g, Proteins: 17.4 g

38. Cheese and Yogurt Bowl

Preparation Time: 10 minutes *Cooking Time: 0 minutes* *Servings: 4*

Ingredients:
- ½ cup plain fat-free Greek yogurt
- ½ cup low-fat cottage cheese
- 2 tsp extra-virgin olive oil
- ¼ tsp ground cinnamon
- ¼ cup fresh strawberries, hulled and sliced
- ¼ cup fresh blueberries
- ¼ cup fresh raspberries
- 2 tbsp walnuts, chopped

Directions:
1. Add the yogurt, cheese, oil, and cinnamon in a large bowl, and mix until well combined.
2. Divide the yogurt mixture into 2 serving bowls.
3. Top with berries and walnuts, and serve immediately.

Nutrition Facts (per serving):
Calories: 224 kcal, Fats: 17.6 g, Carbs: 6.1 g, Proteins: 9.9 g

39. Cherry Berry Bulgur Bowl

Preparation Time: 15 minutes *Cooking Time: 15 minutes* *Servings: 5*

Ingredients:
- 1 cup medium-grind bulgur
- 2 cups water
- A pinch salt
- 1 cup halved and pitted cherries or 1 cup canned cherries, drained
- ½ cup raspberries
- ½ cup blackberries
- 1 tbsp cherry jam
- 2 cups plain whole-milk yogurt

Directions:
1. Mix the bulgur, water, and salt in a medium saucepan. Do this in medium heat. Bring to a boil.
2. Reduce the heat to low and simmer, partially covered, for 12 to 15 minutes or until the bulgur is almost tender. Cover, and let stand for 5 minutes to finish cooking. Do this after removing the pan from the heat.
3. While the bulgur is cooking, combine the raspberries and blackberries in a medium bowl. Stir the cherry jam into the fruit.
4. When the bulgur is tender, divide it among four bowls. Top each bowl with ½ cup yogurt and an equal amount of the berry mixture, and serve.

Nutrition Facts (per serving):
Calories: 216 kcal, Fats: 3.7 g, Carbs: 37.8 g, Proteins: 8.1 g

Preparation Time: 10 minutes   *Cooking Time: 2 minutes*   *Servings: 4*

Ingredients:

- 4 pieces (6-inch) pitas, cut into halves
- 2 cups roasted chicken breast skinless, boneless, and sliced
- ¼ cup red onion, thinly sliced
- ½ tsp dried oregano
- ½ cup Greek yogurt, plain
- ½ cup plum tomato, chopped
- ½ cup cucumber peeled and chopped
- ½ cup (2 oz) feta cheese, crumbled
- 1 tbsp olive oil, extra-virgin, divided
- 1 tbsp fresh dill, chopped
- 1 cup iceberg lettuce, shredded
- 1 ¼ tsp minced garlic, bottled, divided

Directions:

1. In a small mixing bowl, combine the yogurt, cheese, 1 teaspoon of olive oil, and ¼ teaspoon of garlic until well mixed.
2. In a large skillet, heat the remaining olive oil over medium-high heat. Add the remaining garlic and the oregano; sauté for 20 seconds.
3. Add the chicken; cook for about 2 minutes or until the chicken is heated through.
4. Put ¼ cup of chicken into each pita half; top with two tablespoons of yogurt mix, two tablespoons of lettuce, one tablespoon of tomato, and one tablespoon of cucumber. Divide the onion between the pita halves.

Nutrition Facts (per serving):
Calories: 300 kcal, Fats: 11.3 g, Sodium: 595 mg, Carbs: 31.6 g, Proteins: 15.7 g

41. Colorful Scrambled Eggs

Preparation Time: 10 minutes *Cooking Time: 5 minutes* *Servings: 3*

Ingredients:
- 4 eggs
- ⅛ tsp salt
- ⅛ tsp pepper
- 1 tbsp olive oil
- 2 tbsp red bell pepper, chopped
- 1 garlic clove, chopped
- 1 tsp chives, chopped

Directions:
1. Mix eggs, pepper, and salt; set aside.
2. In a large skillet, heat oil; add red bell pepper and garlic. Over medium heat, cook for 5 minutes, stirring constantly.
3. Add egg mixture and chives to skillet; cook and stir over low heat until eggs are cooked.

Nutrition Facts (per serving):
Calories: 182 kcal, Fats: 15.9 g, Carbs: 1.3 g, Proteins: 8.6 g

42. Corn Meal Mush With Polish Sausage

Preparation Time: 10 minutes *Cooking Time: 10 minutes* *Servings: 10*

Ingredients:
- 16 oz cornmeal mush, refrigerated
- 16 oz Polish sausage, skinless
- ½ tsp butter
- Stevia

Directions:
1. Cut both mush and sausage into 1-inch slices; set aside.
2. In a skillet, melt butter. Add mush as you lay the slices side by side. Cook until softened and lightly browned on one side for about 10 minutes; turn over to brown the other.
3. After turning the mush over to brown both sides, add the sausage to the skillet; place around the edges of the skillet and between the mush slices to warm throughout (you may also use a separate skillet to heat sausage).
4. Serve with maple syrup drizzled on top.

Nutrition Facts (per serving):
Calories: 317 kcal, Fats: 14.1 g, Carbs: 36.9 g, Proteins: 10.8 g

43. Egg and Black Beans Scramble

Preparation Time: 8 minutes   *Cooking Time: 15 minutes*   *Servings: 2*

Ingredients:
- 1 tsp olive oil
- 5 ½ oz canned cannellini beans, rinsed and drained
- 1 shallot, sliced thinly
- 2 eggs, lightly beaten
- Ground black pepper, as needed
- 1 tbsp fresh parsley, chopped

Directions:
1. In a nonstick sauté pan, heat the oil over low heat and cook the beans and shallot for about 10 minutes, stirring occasionally.
2. Add the eggs and black pepper, then cook for about 3 to 5 minutes or until done completely, stirring continuously.
3. Remove from the heat and serve immediately with the parsley garnishing.

Nutrition Facts (per serving):
Calories: 240 kcal, Fats: 19.8 g, Carbs: 6.3 g, Proteins: 9.8 g

44. Eggs With Spinach

Preparation Time: 10 minutes   *Cooking Time: 22 minutes*   *Servings: 2*

Ingredients:
- 6 cups of fresh baby spinach
- 2 to 3 tbsp filtered water
- 4 eggs
- Ground black pepper, as needed
- 2 to 3 tbsp feta cheese, crumbled
- 2 tsp fresh chives, minced

Nutrition Facts (per serving):
Calories: 210 kcal,
Fats: 13.5 g, Carbs: 3.2 g,
Proteins: 18.8 g

Directions:
1. Preheat your oven to 400°F.
2. Lightly grease 2 small baking dishes.
3. In a nonstick frying pan, put the spinach and water over medium heat and cook for about 3–4 minutes, stirring occasionally.
4. Remove from the heat and drain the excess water completely.
5. Divide the spinach into prepared baking dishes evenly.
6. Carefully crack 2 eggs in each baking dish over the spinach.
7. Sprinkle with black pepper and top with feta cheese evenly.
8. Arrange the baking dishes onto a large cookie sheet.
9. Bake for approximately 15 to 18 minutes or until the egg is set.
10. Remove from the oven and serve hot with the garnishing of chives.

45. Mushroom-Egg Casserole

Preparation Time: 10 minutes   *Cooking Time: 30 minutes*   *Servings: 3*

Ingredients:

- ½ cup mushrooms, chopped
- ½ yellow onion, diced
- 4 eggs, beaten
- 1 tbsp coconut flakes
- ½ tsp chili pepper
- 1 oz Cheddar cheese, shredded
- 1 tsp canola oil

Directions:

1. Pour canola oil into a skillet and preheat well.
2. Add the mushrooms and onion, then roast for 5-8 minutes or until the vegetables are light brown.
3. Transfer the cooked vegetables to a casserole mold.
4. Add coconut flakes, chili pepper, and Cheddar cheese.
5. Then add the eggs and stir well.
6. Bake the casserole for 15 minutes at 360°F.

Nutrition Facts (per serving):
Calories: 191 kcal, Fats: 14.9 g, Carbs: 2 g, Proteins: 12.3 g

---

46. Pineapple, Macha & Beet Chia Pudding

Preparation Time: 10 minutes   *Cooking Time: 0 minutes*   *Servings: 10*

Ingredients:

- 1 cup chia seeds
- 1 tsp raw honey
- 2 cups almond milk
- 1 tsp matcha green tea powder
- 2 tbsp fresh beetroot juice
- 1 whole pineapple
- 1 cup freshly squeezed lemon juice
- 1 knob of fresh ginger
- Toasted almonds and figs to serve

Directions:

Green chia pudding layer:

1. Add the half of chia seeds, raw honey, almond milk, and matcha green tea powder to the blender and until very smooth; transfer to a bowl.

Beetroot layer:

2. Blend beetroot and ginger with the remaining chia seeds, raw honey, vanilla, and coconut milk until very smooth; transfer to a separate bowl. In a food processor, puree the fresh pineapple until fine.
3. To assemble, layer the chia pudding in the bottom of the serving glasses, followed by the pureed pineapple and then the beetroot layer. Top with figs and toasted almonds for a crunchy finish.

Nutrition Facts (per serving):
Calories: 165 kcal, Fats: 7.5 g, Carbs: 20.1 g, Proteins: 4.5 g

---

47. Sweet Potato and Rosemary Waffles

Preparation Time: 10 minutes   *Cooking Time: 20 minutes*   *Servings: 2*

Ingredients:

- 1 medium sweet potato; peeled, grated, and squeezed
- ½ tsp dried rosemary, crushed
- Pinch red pepper flakes, crushed
- Ground black pepper, as needed

Directions:

1. Preheat the waffle iron and then grease it.
2. In a large bowl, add all ingredients and mix until well combined.
3. Place half of the mixture in the preheated waffle iron.
4. Cook for about 8–10 minutes or until waffles become golden brown.
5. Repeat with the remaining mixture.
6. Serve warm.

Nutrition Facts (per serving):
Calories: 205 kcal, Fats: 1.2 g, Carbs: 44.8 g, Proteins: 3 g

---

48. Tahini Pine Nuts Toast

Preparation Time: 10 minutes   *Cooking Time: 0 minutes*   *Servings: 2*

Ingredients:

- 2 whole wheat bread slices, toasted
- 1 tsp water
- 1 tbsp tahini paste
- 2 tsp feta cheese, crumbled
- Juice ½ lemon
- 2 tsp pine nuts
- A pinch black pepper

Directions:

1. In a bowl, mix the tahini with the water and the lemon juice, whisk really well, and spread over the toasted bread slices.
2. Top each serving with the remaining ingredients and serve for breakfast.

Nutrition Facts (per serving):
Calories: 196 kcal, Fats: 10.2 g, Carbs: 19 g, Proteins: 7.1 g

49. Vanilla Crepes

Preparation Time: 10 minutes   *Cooking Time: 18 minutes*   *Servings: 4*

Ingredients:

- 2 tbsp arrowroot powder
- 2 tbsp almond flour
- ½ tsp ground cinnamon
- 4 eggs
- 1 tsp vanilla extract
- Olive oil cooking spray

Directions:

1. In a bowl, add the arrowroot powder, almond flour, and cinnamon, and mix well.
2. In another bowl, add the eggs and vanilla extract and beat until well combined.
3. Add the egg mixture into the bowl of the flour mixture and mix until well combined.
4. Lightly grease a large nonstick sauté pan with cooking spray and heat over medium-high heat.
5. Add the desired amount of mixture and tilt the pan to spread in an even and thin layer.
6. Cook for about 1 minute or until the bottom becomes golden brown.
7. Carefully flip and cook for about 1 minute more or until golden brown.
8. Repeat with the remaining mixture.
9. Serve warm.

Nutrition Facts (per serving):
Calories: 141 kcal, Fats: 10.9 g, Carbs: 1.3 g, Proteins: 8.9 g

CHAPTER 7

Snacks Recipes

50. Feta Tomato Sea Bass

Preparation Time: 10 minutes   *Cooking Time: 8 minutes*   *Servings: 4*

Ingredients:

- 4 sea bass fillets
- 2 cups water
- 1 tbsp olive oil
- 1 tsp garlic, minced
- 1 tsp basil, chopped
- 1 tsp parsley, chopped
- ½ cup feta cheese, crumbled
- 1 cup can tomatoes, diced
- Pepper
- Salt

Directions:

1. Season the fish fillets with pepper and salt.
2. Pour 2 cups of water into the instant pot, then place a steamer rack in the pot.
3. Place fish fillets on the steamer rack in the pot.
4. Seal the pot with a lid and cook on high for 5 minutes
5. Once done, release pressure using quick release. Remove the lid.
6. Remove the fish fillets from the pot and clean it.
7. Add oil into the inner container of the instant pot and set it on sauté mode.
8. Add garlic and sauté for 1 minute.
9. Add tomatoes, parsley, and basil, stir well, and cook for 1 minute.
10. Add fish fillets and top with crumbled cheese, then cook for a minute.
11. Serve and enjoy.

Nutrition Facts (per serving):
Calories: 204 kcal, Fats: 9.8 g, Carbs: 1.4 g, Proteins: 27.7 g

51. Garlicky Green Beans Stir Fry

Preparation Time: 25 minutes   *Cooking Time: 10 minutes*   *Servings: 4*

Ingredients:

- 2 tbsp Peanut oil
- 1 lb fresh green beans
- 2 tbsp garlic, chopped
- Salt and red chili pepper to taste
- ½ yellow onion, slivered

Directions:

1. Heat the peanut oil in a wok over high heat and add garlic and onions.
2. Sauté for about 4 minutes; add beans, salt, and red chili pepper.
3. Sauté for about 3 minutes and add a little water.
4. Cover with a lid and cook on low heat for about 5 minutes
5. Dish out into a bowl and serve hot.

Nutrition Facts (per serving):
Calories: 239 kcal, Fats: 15.5 g, Carbs: 14 g, Proteins: 10.8 g

52. Green Tea Smoothie

Preparation Time: 10 minutes   *Cooking Time: 10 minutes*   *Servings: 2*

Ingredients:

- 3 tbsp green tea powder
- 1 cup grapes, white
- ½ cup kale, finely chopped
- 1 tbsp honey
- ½ tsp fresh mint, ground
- 1 cup water

Directions:

1. Rinse the grapes under cold running water. Drain and remove the pits. Set aside.
2. Place kale in a large colander and wash thoroughly under cold running water. Drain well and finely chop it into small pieces. Set aside.
3. Combine green tea powder with 2 tbsp of hot water. Soak for 2 minutes Set aside.
4. Now, combine grapes, kale, honey, mint, and water in a blender and process until well combined. Stir in the water and tea mixture.
5. Refrigerate for 30 minutes before serving.
6. Enjoy!

Nutrition Facts (per serving):
Calories: 127 kcal, Carbs: 21.3 g, Proteins: 8 g, Fats: 1 g

53. Grilled Shrimp Kabobs

Preparation Time: 10 minutes   *Cooking Time: 30 minutes*   *Servings: 4*

Ingredients:

- 1 ½ cup whole-wheat dry breadcrumbs
- 1 garlic clove, finely minced or pressed
- 1 tsp dried basil leaves
- ¼ cup olive oil
- 2 lb shrimp, peeled and deveined, leaving the tails on
- 2 tbsp vegetable oil
- 2 tsp dried parsley flakes
- Salt and pepper
- 16 skewers, soaked for at least 20 minutes in water or until ready to use if using wooden

Directions:

1. Rinse the shrimp and dry them.
2. Put the vegetables and the olive oil in a re-sealable plastic bag, add the shrimp, and toss to coat with the oil mixture.
3. Add the breadcrumbs, parsley, garlic, basil, salt, and pepper; toss to coat with the dry mix.
4. Seal the bag, and refrigerate for 1 hour. Thread the shrimp on the skewers.
5. Cook on a preheated grill for about 2 minutes on each side or until golden, making sure not to overcook.

Nutrition Facts (per serving):
Calories: 444 kcal, Fats: 18.3 g, Carbs: 34.1 g, Proteins: 35.8 g

54. Maple-Mashed Sweet Potatoes

Preparation Time: 5 minutes   *Cooking Time: 10 minutes*   *Servings: 4*

Ingredients:

- 1 lb sweet potatoes
- 1 cup carrots, thinly sliced
- 2 tbsp maple syrup
- ¼ tsp nutmeg
- ¼ tsp fresh ground pepper
- 4 cups water

Nutrition Facts (per serving):
Calories: 295 kcal, Fats: 1.1 g, Carbs: 67.1 g, Proteins: 4.2 g

Directions:

1. Wash and clean the sweet potatoes.
2. Peel and cut them into small chunks.
3. In a large bowl, pour water and bring it to a boil.
4. Put the carrots and sweet potatoes into it.
5. Reduce the heat and cook for about 10 minutes until the carrots and sweet potatoes become soft.
6. Drain the vegetables using a colander and put them into a bowl.
7. Mas the vegetables until smooth.
8. Sprinkle ground pepper and nutmeg into it and stir.
9. Drizzle maple syrup over it and stir.

55. Pureed Classic Egg Salad

Preparation Time: 5 minutes　　*Cooking Time: 2 minutes*　　*Servings: 2*

Ingredients:
- 2 eggs, hard-boiled
- 1 tbsp Low-fat mayonnaise
- 1 tbsp Greek yogurt, plain

Directions:
1. Cut the boiled eggs into even portions.
2. Put the egg slices into a food mixer and chop them.
3. Add salt, mayonnaise, and Greek yogurt as the seasonings to the eggs
4. Mix finely as far as the egg salad becomes smooth.

Nutrition Facts (per serving):
Calories: 141 kcal, Fats: 12.3 g, Carbs: 0.4 g, Proteins: 7.2 g

56. Yellow Pepper Tapenade

Preparation Time: 10 minutes　　*Cooking Time: 0 minutes*　　*Servings: 3*

Ingredients:
- ½ cup parmesan, grated
- 1 ½ tbsp lemon juice
- ½ cup parsley, chopped
- ½ cup capers drained
- 6 oz roasted yellow peppers, chopped
- 12 oz canned artichokes, drained and chopped
- 2 tbsp olive oil
- 1 garlic clove, minced

Directions:
1. Combine the yellow peppers with the parmesan and the rest of the ingredients in your blender, and pulse well.
2. Divide into cups and serve as a snack.

Nutrition Facts (per serving):
Calories: 36 kcal, Fats: 19.2 g, Carbs: 6.7 g, Proteins: 8.9 g

57. Salmon and Broccoli

Preparation Time: 10 minutes　　　*Cooking Time: 20 minutes*　　　*Servings: 4*

Ingredients:

- 2 tbsp balsamic vinegar
- 1 broccoli head, florets separated
- 4 pieces salmon fillets, skinless
- 1 onion, roughly chopped
- 2 tbsp olive oil
- Sea salt and black pepper to the taste

Directions:

1. In a baking dish, combine the salmon with the broccoli and the rest of the ingredients, introduce in the oven, and bake at 390°F for 20 minutes.
2. Divide the mix between plates and serve.

Nutrition Facts (per serving):
Calories: 233 kcal, Fats: 15.2 g, Carbs: 5.3 g, Proteins: 18.8 g

58. Savory Cheese Biscuits

Preparation Time: 5 minutes　　　*Cooking Time: 15 minutes*　　　*Servings: 4*

Ingredients:

- 1 cup almond flour
- ¼ cup shredded Parmesan cheese
- ¼ cup shredded Cheddar cheese
- 2 tsp baking powder
- 2 tsp garlic powder
- ½ tsp salt
- 2 large eggs

Directions:

1. Preheat the oven to 350°F. Line a large baking sheet with parchment paper and set it aside.
2. Add the almond flour, parmesan cheese, cheddar cheese, baking powder, garlic powder, and salt in a large bowl. Mix well. Add the eggs and combine.
3. Scoop a heaping tablespoon of the mixture onto the baking sheet. Using a spatula, flatten the batter slightly into about 2-inch circles. Repeat, placing biscuits about an inch apart. This should yield 8 small biscuits.
4. Bake for 15 minutes or until the top of the biscuits is slightly golden brown. Serve warm.

Nutrition Facts (per serving):
Calories: 237 kcal, Proteins: 13 g, Fats: 19.3 g, Carbs: 2.8 g

CHAPTER 8

Appetizers Recipes

59. Citrus, Fennel, and Avocado Bowl

Preparation Time: 10 minutes   *Cooking Time: 0 minutes*   *Servings: 6*

Ingredients:

- 3 tbsp olive oil
- 1 lemon juice
- 1 tbsp fresh mint, chopped
- 2 tbsp fresh parsley, chopped
- 1 tsp kosher salt
- ½ tsp black pepper
- 6 cups arugula
- 2 oranges, peeled and chopped
- 2 blood oranges, peeled and chopped
- 1 ruby-red grapefruit, peeled and chopped
- 1 bulb fennel, quartered and sliced
- 2 avocados, halved, pitted, and sliced

Directions:

1. Mix black pepper, salt, parsley, mint, lemon juice, and oil in a small bowl.
2. Add the arugula into this mixture, toss well, then spread it onto a platter.
3. Top with the remaining ingredients and serve.

Nutrition Facts (per serving):
Calories: 310 kcal, Fats: 25.4 g, Carbs: 14.8 g, Proteins: 5.4 g

60. Orange Couscous

Preparation Time: 5 minutes   *Cooking Time: 10 minutes*   *Servings: 1*

Ingredients:
- ¼ cup couscous
- 1 tsp Italian seasonings
- ¼ cup water
- 4 tbsp orange juice
- ⅓ orange, chopped
- ⅓ tsp salt
- ½ tsp butter

Directions:
1. Pour water and orange juice into a pan. Add Italian seasoning, orange, and salt. Bring the liquid to a boil and remove it from the heat.
2. Add couscous and butter. Stir well and close the lid. Leave the couscous to rest for 10 minutes

Nutrition Facts (per serving):
Calories: 150 kcal, Fats: 4.4 g, Carbs: 24.5 g, Proteins: 2.8 g

61. Paprika Couscous

Preparation Time: 15 minutes   *Cooking Time: 10 minutes*   *Servings: 4*

Ingredients:
- 3 ½ cups chicken stock
- ½ cup mascarpone
- 1 tsp salt
- 1 cup couscous
- 1 tsp ground paprika

Directions:
1. Place mascarpone and chicken stock in the pan and bring the liquid to a boil. Add salt and ground paprika. Stir gently and simmer for 1 minute.
2. Remove the liquid from the heat and add couscous. Stir well and close the lid. Leave the couscous for 10 minutes. Stir the cooked side dish well before serving.

Nutrition Facts (per serving):
Calories: 289 kcal, Fats: 24.3 g, Carbs: 10.2 g, Proteins: 7.6 g

62. Rainbow Skewers

Preparation Time: 10 minutes   *Cooking Time: 10 minutes*   *Servings: 5*

Ingredients:

For the Lemon-Parsley Dressing:

- ⅓ cup lemon juice
- 1 lemon zest
- 1 tbsp Dijon mustard
- ½ cup olive oil
- ¼ cup chopped fresh parsley
- ¾ tsp garlic powder
- 1 pinch cayenne pepper
- Salt and black pepper

For the Skewers:

- 3 red onions, cut into large pieces
- 2 summer squash, sliced
- 4 orange bell peppers, cut into squares
- 2 pints cherry tomatoes
- 2 zucchinis, sliced
- 1 eggplant, cut into large cubes
- Salt and black pepper, to taste
- 2 tbsp fresh parsley, chopped

Directions:

1. Mix all the ingredients for the lemon parsley dressing in a bowl.
2. Assemble the onions and all the veggies on the wooden skewers alternatingly.
3. Sprinkle black pepper, salt, and parsley over the skewers.
4. Set a grill pan over medium heat and grill the skewers for 5 minutes on each side.
5. Top with the lemon dressing and serve.

Nutrition Facts (per serving):
Calories: 309 kcal, Fats: 21.3 g, Carbs: 23.2 g, Proteins: 6.2 g

63. Croutons

Ingredients:

- 1 tbsp olive oil
- 4 sourdough bread sliced, cut into small cubes
- Salt and black pepper, to taste

Directions:

1. Toss bread cubes with oil, black pepper, and salt in a skillet.
2. Sauté these cubes for 4 minutes on medium heat until golden brown.
3. Serve.

Nutrition Facts (per serving):
Calories: 180 kcal, Fats: 3.8 g, Carbs: 32.4 g, Proteins: 4.1 g

64. Broccoli Rabe and Burrata

Ingredients:

- 1 bunch broccoli rabe
- 1 to 2 tbsp olive oil
- 2 garlic cloves, sliced
- ¼ tsp red pepper flakes
- 4 oz burrata mozzarella
- ½ tbsp fresh lemon juice
- 2 tbsp crushed, toasted pistachios
- Flaky sea salt to serve
- Water

Directions:

1. Boil the broccoli in salted water for about 3 minutes, then drain.
2. Sauté the garlic with 2 tbsp oil in a skillet for 30 seconds.
3. Add in the broccoli rabe and red pepper flakes, then cook for 5 minutes
4. Transfer the rabe onto a plate and garnish with the rest of the ingredients.
5. Serve.

Nutrition Facts (per serving):
Calories: 258 kcal, Fats: 20.2 g, Carbs: 6.6 g, Proteins: 12.4 g

65. Lemon-Pinoli Zucchini

Preparation Time: 10 minutes   *Cooking Time: 0 minutes*   *Servings: 3*

Ingredients:
- 1 cups orecchiette pasta
- 2 small zucchinis, sliced
- 1-pint cherry tomatoes, cut in half
- Grated zest and juice of 2 lemons
- ¼ cup olive oil
- Salt and black pepper, to taste
- 1 ½ cup crumbled feta cheese
- ½ cup fresh basil leaves, chopped
- ½ cup pine nuts

Directions:
1. Cook the pasta as per the instructions on the package.
2. When it is cooked, drain and rinse under cold water, then set it aside.
3. Mix the tomatoes with zucchini, lemon peel, salt, pepper, and lemon juice in a bowl.
4. Stir in the cooked pasta and toss well.
5. Add the basil and feta cheese.
6. Top with pine nuts and serve immediately.

Nutrition Facts (per serving):
Calories: 426 kcal, Fats: 19.8 g, Carbs: 49.4 g, Proteins: 14.2 g

66. Herbed Olives

Preparation Time: 10 minutes   *Cooking Time: 0 minutes*   *Servings: 4*

Ingredients:
- 3 cups olives
- 2 tsp olive oil
- ⅛ tsp dried oregano
- ⅛ tsp dried basil
- 1 garlic clove, crushed
- Black pepper, to taste

Directions:
1. Mix the olives with oregano, oil, garlic, basil, and pepper in a bowl.
2. Serve and enjoy.

Nutrition Facts (per serving):
Calories: 214 kcal, Fats: 22.3 g, Carbs: 2.2 g, Proteins: 1.1 g

67. Roasted Beet Hummus

Preparation Time: 10 minutes   *Cooking Time: 0 minutes*   *Servings: 4*

Ingredients:

- 1 (15 oz) can chickpeas, rinsed
- 8 oz roasted beets, chopped
- ¼ cup tahini
- ¼ cup olive oil
- ¼ cup lemon juice
- 1 garlic clove
- 1 tsp ground cumin
- ½ tsp salt

Directions:

1. Blend the chickpeas with the tahini, oil, beets, garlic, salt, and cumin in a blender.
2. Serve with pita chips.

Nutrition Facts (per serving):
Calories: 231 kcal, Fats: 10.5 g, Carbs: 23.8 g, Proteins: 10.5 g

68. Ground Chicken Lettuce Wraps

Preparation Time: 15 minutes   *Cooking Time: 15 minutes*   *Servings: 8*

Ingredients:

For the Chicken:
- 2 tbsp avocado oil
- 1 small onion, chopped finely
- 1 tsp fresh ginger, minced
- 2 garlic cloves, minced
- 1 ¼ lb ground chicken
- Salt and ground black pepper, as required

For the Wraps:
- 10 romaine lettuce leaves
- 1 ½ cup carrot, peeled and julienned
- 2 tbsp fresh parsley, chopped finely
- 2 tbsp fresh lime juice

Directions:

1. Heat the oil over medium heat in a wok and sauté the onion, ginger, and garlic for about 4-5 minutes.
2. Add the ground chicken, salt, and black pepper, and cook over medium-high heat for about 7-9 minutes, breaking up the meat into smaller pieces with a wooden spoon.
3. Remove from the heat and set aside to cool.
4. Arrange the lettuce leaves onto serving plates.
5. Place the cooked chicken over each lettuce leaf and top with carrot and cilantro.
6. Drizzle with lime juice and serve immediately.

Nutrition Facts (per serving):
Calories: 289 kcal, Fats: 12.5 g, Carbs: 12.8 g, Proteins: 31.2 g

69. Pan-Fried Trout

Preparation Time: 15 minutes　　*Cooking Time: 10 minutes*　　*Servings: 8*

Ingredients:
- 1 ¼ lb trout fillets
- ¼ tsp black pepper
- ¼ cup minced cilantro, or parsley
- Vegetable cooking spray
- ⅓ cup white, or yellow, cornmeal
- ¼ tsp anise seeds
- Lemon wedges

Directions:
1. Coat the fish with combined cornmeal, spices, and cilantro, pressing it gently into the fish. Spray a large skillet with cooking spray; heat over medium heat until hot.
2. Add the fish and cook until it is tender and flakes with a fork, about 5 minutes on each side. Serve with lemon wedges.

Nutrition Facts (per serving):
Calories: 193 kcal, Carbs: 5 g, Fats: 6.7 g, Proteins: 28.2 g

70. Savory Pita Chips

Preparation Time: 10 minutes　　*Cooking Time: 10 minutes*　　*Servings: 3*

Ingredients:
- 3 pitas
- ¼ cup olive oil
- ¼ cup zaatar

Directions:
1. Preheat the oven to 450°F.
2. Cut the pitas into 2-inch pieces and place them in a large bowl.
3. Drizzle the pitas with olive oil, sprinkle with zaatar, and toss to coat.
4. Spread the pitas on a baking sheet, and bake for 8 to 10 minutes or until lightly browned and crunchy.
5. Let the pita chips cool before removing them from the baking sheet. Store in an airtight container for up to 1 month.

Nutrition Facts (per serving):
Calories: 341kcal, Carbs: 31.5 g, Fats: 21.4 g, Proteins: 5.9 g

71. Protein Pumpkin Spiced Donuts

Preparation Time: 10 minutes   *Cooking Time: 15 minutes*   *Servings: 6*

Ingredients:
- 1 cup oat flour.
- ¾ cup xylitol.
- 1 scoop powdered vanilla protein.
- 1 tbsp ground flaxseed.
- 1 tbsp ground cinnamon.
- 2 tsp baking powder.
- 1 tsp sea salt.
- 3 beaten eggs.
- ½ cup canned pumpkin.
- 1 tbsp melted coconut oil.
- 2 tsp pure vanilla.
- 1 tsp apple cider vinegar

For the Frosting:
- ½ cup whipped cream cheese
- ½ tsp liquid stevia.

Directions:
1. Place the xylitol, oat flour, ground flaxseed, powdered protein, baking powder, ground cinnamon, and a dash of sea salt in a large bowl. Preheat your oven to 350°F.
2. Add the egg (beaten) into another bowl (large) along with the pumpkin (canned), pure vanilla, vinegar, and coconut oil (melted).
3. Whisk until mixed (evenly), then pour the mixture into the flour. Stir until thoroughly mixed.
4. Use cooking spray to grease a large donut pan.
5. Pour the batter into the donut pan (greased).
6. Place into the oven and bake for approximately 10 minutes until thoroughly baked.
7. Remove from the heat and set the donuts on a wire rack to cool.
8. Add in the cream cheese (whipped) and liquid stevia in a small bowl, then whisk until it becomes smooth.
9. Frost the donuts using the frosting and serve with a sprinkle of cinnamon (ground) over the top.

Nutrition Facts (per serving):
Calories: 289 kcal, Proteins: 10.6 g, Carbs: 30.8 g, Fats: 13.2 g

72. Artichoke Skewers

Preparation Time: 10 minutes   *Cooking Time: 0 minutes*   *Servings: 2*

Ingredients:
- 4 prosciutto slices
- 4 artichoke hearts, canned
- 4 kalamata olives
- 4 cherry tomatoes
- ¼ tsp cayenne pepper
- ¼ tsp sunflower oil

Directions:
1. Skewer the prosciutto slices, artichoke hearts, kalamata olives, and cherry tomatoes on the wooden skewers.
2. Sprinkle the skewers with sunflower oil and cayenne pepper.

Nutrition Facts (per serving):
Calories: 162 kcal, Fats: 9 g, Carbs: 5.1 g, Proteins: 15.1 g

73. Polenta Cups Recipe

Preparation Time: 10 minutes   *Cooking Time: 20 minutes*   *Servings: 3*

Ingredients:

- 1 cup yellow cornmeal
- 1 garlic clove, minced
- ½ tsp fresh thyme, minced or ¼ tsp dried thyme
- ½ tsp salt
- ¼ cup feta cheese, crumbled
- ¼ tsp pepper
- 2 tbsp fresh basil, chopped
- 4 cups water
- 4 plum tomatoes, finely chopped

Directions:

1. Bring the water and salt to a boil in a heavy, large saucepan; reduce the heat to a gentle boil. Slowly whisk in the cornmeal; cook, stirring with a wooden spoon, for about 15 to 20 minutes, or until the polenta is thick and pulls away cleanly from the sides of the pan. Remove from the heat; stir in the pepper and the thyme.
2. Grease a miniature muffin cup with cooking spray. Spoon a heaping tablespoon of the polenta mixture into each muffin cup.
3. With the back of a spoon, make an indentation in the center of each; cover and chill until the mixture is set.
4. Meanwhile, combine the feta cheese, tomatoes, garlic, and basil in a small-sized bowl.
5. Unmold the chilled polenta cups, and place them on an ungreased baking sheet. Top each with one heaping tablespoon of the feta mixture. Broil the cups 4 inches from the heat source for about 5 to 7 minutes or until heated through.

Nutrition Facts (per serving):
Calories: 200 kcal, Carbs: 35.5 g, Fats: 3.7 g, Proteins: 6.3 g

74. Strawberry Oatmeal

Preparation Time: 5 minutes   *Cooking Time: 5 minutes*   *Servings: 4*

Ingredients:

- 2 cups water
- ½ tsp Ground cinnamon
- 2 cups old-fashioned oats
- ½ tsp salt
- 8 strawberries, chopped
- 2 cups milk

Directions:

1. Save a few strawberry slices for garnishing.
2. Add the remaining ingredients to a cooker. Secure the lid and press the multigrain option.
3. Adjust the time to 5 minutes and let it cook.
4. After the signal, release the pressure and remove the lid.
5. Serve with the chopped strawberries on top.

Nutrition Facts (per serving):
Calories: 231 kcal, Fats: 7.3 g, Proteins: 10.2 g, Carbs: 30.3 g

CHAPTER 9

Salads and Fruits Recipes

75. Tofu Sesame Skewers With Warm Kale Salad

Preparation Time: 2 hours   *Cooking Time: 25 minutes*   *Servings: 8*

Ingredients:

- 14 oz firm tofu
- 4 tsp Sesame oil
- Lemon, juiced
- Sugar-free soy sauce
- Garlic powder
- Coconut flour
- ½ cup sesame seeds

For the Warm Kale Salad:

- 2 cups chopped kale
- 2 tsp + 2 tsp Olive oil
- A small white onion, thinly sliced
- 3 garlic cloves, minced
- 1 cup sliced white mushrooms
- 1 tsp chopped rosemary
- Salt and black pepper to season
- 1 tbsp Balsamic vinegar

Directions:

1. Mix sesame oil, lemon juice, soy sauce, garlic powder, and coconut flour in a bowl.
2. Wrap the tofu in a paper towel, squeeze out as much liquid from it as possible, and cut it into strips.
3. Stick on the skewers, height-wise.
4. Place onto a plate, pour the soy sauce mixture over, and turn in the sauce to be adequately coated.
5. Heat the griddle pan over high heat.
6. Pour the sesame seeds into a plate and roll the tofu skewers in the seeds for a generous coat.
7. Grill the tofu in the griddle pan to be golden brown on both sides, about 12 minutes.
8. Heat two tablespoons of olive oil in a skillet over medium heat and sauté onion to begin browning for 10 minutes with continuous stirring.
9. Add the remaining olive oil and mushrooms.
10. Continue cooking for 10 minutes. Add garlic, rosemary, salt, pepper, and balsamic vinegar.
11. Cook for 1 minute.
12. Put the kale in a salad bowl; when the onion mixture is ready, pour it on the kale and toss it well.
13. Serve the tofu skewers with the warm kale salad and a peanut butter dipping sauce.

Nutrition Facts (per serving):
Calories: 304 kcal, Fats: 28.4 g, Carbs: 4.3 g, Proteins: 7.9 g

76. Ground Turkey Salad

Preparation Time: 20 minutes   *Cooking Time: 13 minutes*   *Servings: 4*

Ingredients:

- 1 pound ground turkey
- 2 tbsp olive oil
- Salt and ground black pepper, as required
- ¼ cup water
- ½ English cucumber, chopped
- 4 cups green cabbage, shredded
- ½ cup fresh mint leaves, chopped
- 2 tbsp fresh lime juice
- ¼ cup walnuts, chopped

Directions:

1. Heat oil in a large wok over medium-high heat and cook the turkey for about 6-8 minutes, breaking up the pieces with a spatula.
2. Stir in the water and cook for about 4-5 minutes or until almost all the liquid is evaporated.
3. Remove from the heat and transfer the turkey into a bowl.
4. Set the bowl aside to cool completely.
5. Add the vegetables, mint, and lime juice to a large serving bowl, then mix well.
6. Add the cooked turkey and stir to combine.
7. Serve immediately.

Nutrition Facts (per serving):
Calories: 212 kcal, Fats: 12.8 g, Carbs: 5.4 g, Proteins: 18.7 g

77. Arugula Green Beans Salad

Preparation Time: 10 minutes   *Cooking Time: 25 minutes*   *Servings: 4*

Ingredients:

For the Salad:

- 2 handfuls arugula
- 4 tbsp capers
- 15 oz lentils, cooked
- 15 oz green kidney beans

For the Dressing:

- 1 tbsp balsamic vinegar
- 1 tbsp tamari
- 2 tbsp peanut butter
- 1 tbsp caper brine
- 1 tbsp tahini
- 2 tbsp hot sauce

Directions:

1. Begin by placing all the dressing ingredients in a medium bowl and whisk it well until combined.
2. After that, combine the arugula, capers, kidney beans, and lentils in a large bowl. Pour the dressing over it and serve.

Nutrition Facts (per serving):
Calories: 109 kcal, Fats: 3.9 g, Carbs: 11.3 g, Proteins: 7.3 g

78. Blue Cheese Salad With Griddled Pear

Preparation Time: 15 minutes   *Cooking Time: 15 minutes*   *Servings: 4*

Ingredients:

- 1 packet of blue cheese, crumbled
- 1 bag of mixed-leaf salad
- 1 tbsp honey
- 1 tbsp white wine vinegar
- 2 tbsp olive oil
- 4 sliced ripe pears

Directions:

1. Combine the pears and 1 tbsp of olive oil in a large bowl and toss to coat.
2. Heat a frying pan and cook the pears for 1 minute on each side; you will need to do this in batches.
3. Add the rest of the olive oil, honey, and vinegar in a small bowl and whisk to combine.
4. Combine the dressing with the pear, cheese, and mixed leaf salad and toss to combine.
5. Divide onto plates and serve.

Nutrition Facts (per serving):
Calories: 240 kcal, Fats: 17.5 g, Carbs: 18.2 g, Proteins: 4.6 g

79. Broccoli Salad

Preparation Time: 5 minutes   *Cooking Time: 25 minutes*   *Servings: 6*

Ingredients:

- 2 tbsp sherry vinegar
- ¼ cup olive oil
- 2 tsp fresh thyme, chopped
- 1 tsp Dijon mustard
- 1 tsp honey
- Salt to taste
- 8 cups broccoli florets, steamed or roasted
- 2 red onions, sliced thinly
- ½ cup parmesan cheese, shaved
- ¼ cup pecans, toasted and chopped

Directions:

1. Mix the sherry vinegar, olive oil, thyme, mustard, honey, and salt in a bowl.
2. In a serving bowl, combine the broccoli florets and onions.
3. Drizzle the dressing on top.
4. Sprinkle with the pecans and parmesan cheese before serving.

Nutrition Facts (per serving):
Calories: 276 kcal, Fats: 18.4 g, Carbs: 13.9 g, Proteins: 12.2 g

80. Chipotle Steak Salad

Preparation Time: 10 minutes *Cooking Time: 10 minutes* *Servings: 4*

Ingredients:

- ½ cup reduced-fat cheddar cheese, shredded
- 1 tbsp chopped cilantro
- ½ sliced avocado
- 1 diced and seeded tomato
- 1 head washed and torn romaine lettuce
- ½ taco seasoning packet
- 4 lean steaks
- Toppings of choice

Directions:

1. Begin by heating a grill or grill pan to medium. Rub the taco seasoning into the meat, ensuring it is well coated. Set this aside to let it marinate.
2. Once your grill is hot, place steaks on it and cook for five minutes per side until it reaches your desired doneness.
3. Take off the grill and place it on the cutting board. Allow the meat to rest for about four minutes.
4. While steaks are cooking, wash and tear the lettuce. Divide out among four plates.
5. Slice the steaks across the grain and add them on top of the lettuce. Add avocado, tomato, and cilantro. Sprinkle with cheese. Use salsa as the salad dressing if you would like to. Enjoy.

Nutrition Facts (per serving):
Calories: 511 kcal, Fats: 27.6 g, Proteins: 50.4 g, Carbs: 15.7 g

81. Soft Mexican Chicken Salad

Preparation Time: 5 minutes *Cooking Time: 5 minutes* *Servings: 1*

Ingredients:

- 2 tsp juice from jarred salsa
- 1 tsp taco seasoning
- 1 tbsp light mayonnaise
- 1 cup canned chicken, drained

Directions:

1. Put the drained chicken in a bowl. Take a fork and break the chicken into small pieces.
2. Add the mayonnaise to the chicken and combine well. Mash the chicken into the mayonnaise with the fork.
3. Add the salsa juice and taco seasoning to the chicken mixture and continue to mash until everything is well combined. Serve and enjoy.

Nutrition Facts (per serving):
Calories: 296 kcal, Proteins: 33.5 g, Fats: 15.2 g, Carbs: 6.3 g

82. Citrus-Inspired Creamy Garlic & Spinach Salmon

Preparation Time: 5 minutes   *Cooking Time: 5 minutes*   *Servings: 4*

Ingredients:

- 5 tbsp milk
- 1/3 cup mascarpone
- 1 lemon juice
- 1 lemon zest
- 1 thinly sliced lemon
- 6 oz baby spinach
- 2 garlic cloves thinly sliced
- 2 skinless salmon fillets
- 1 tbsp olive oil
- 2 sweet potatoes

Directions:

1. Prepare the oven by heating it to 350°F.
2. Pierce the sweet potatoes with a fork and bake for 40 minutes.
3. Heat ½ a tablespoon of olive oil in a frying pan over medium temperature and brown the salmon on both sides; you don't need to cook it.
4. Put the salmon on a plate, and heat the rest of the oil.
5. Fry the garlic for about 30 seconds. Add the lemon zest, lemon juice, and spinach, and stir to combine.
6. Add 2 tablespoons of milk.
7. Add the mascarpone, and stir to combine until the spinach wilts.
8. Transfer the spinach mixture into an ovenproof dish, add the salmon and the lemon slices, and bake for 10 minutes.
9. Once the sweet potatoes are cooked, scoop the flesh from the skins into a bowl and add the rest of the milk. Mash to combine.
10. Divide the salmon and spinach mixture onto plates, add a scoop of sweet potatoes, and serve.

Nutrition Facts (per serving):
Calories: 324 kcal, Fats: 20 g, Carbs: 21.7 g, Proteins: 14.2 g

83. Corn and Black Bean Salad

⁂ Preparation Time: 30 minutes   *⏲ Cooking Time: 0 minutes*   *☕ Servings: 6*

Ingredients:
- ¼ tsp pepper
- 2 tbsp olive oil
- A salt dash
- 1 tsp minced garlic
- ¼ cup balsamic vinegar
- 2 tbsp minced red onion
- ¼ cup chopped parsley
- 2 16 oz cans drained and rinsed black beans
- 1 cup whole-kernel corn
- Honey
- Lemon juice

Directions:
1. Place the parsley, red onion, black beans, and corn in a large bowl and mix everything.
2. Whisk the pepper, salt, honey, garlic, lemon juice, olive oil, and balsamic vinegar. Make sure that all of the seasonings are mixed well.
3. Pour the dressing you just made over the corn and bean mixture.
4. Toss everything and allow the vegetables to marinate for at least 30 minutes before you serve them, this will allow all the flavors to mix, and the flavor will be much more intense. Enjoy.

Nutrition Facts (per serving):
Calories: 191, Fats: 6.3 g, Proteins: 5.6 g, Carbs: 28 g

84. Snap Pea Salad

⁂ Preparation Time: 1 hour   *⏲ Cooking Time: 0 minutes*   *☕ Servings: 2*

Ingredients:
- 2 tbsp mayonnaise
- ¾ tsp celery seed
- ¼ cup cider vinegar
- 1 tsp yellow mustard
- Salt and pepper to taste
- 4 oz Radishes, sliced thinly
- 12 oz snap peas, sliced thinly

Directions:
1. Combine the mayonnaise, celery seeds, vinegar, mustard, salt, and pepper in a bowl.
2. Stir in the radishes and snap peas.
3. Refrigerate for 30 minutes.

Nutrition Facts (per serving):
Calories: 262 kcal, Fat: 12.5 g, Carbs: 23.3 g, Proteins: 14 g

85. Seven-Layer Mexican Salad

Preparation Time: 20 minutes　　　*Cooking Time: 30 minutes*　　　*Servings: 8*

Ingredients:

For the Dressing:
- ¼ tsp garlic salt
- ½ tsp cumin
- 1 tbsp olive oil
- 2 limes juice
- ½ jalapeño
- ¼ cup cilantro
- 1 avocado

For the Salad:
- 2 green onions chopped,
- 1 cup Low-fat shredded cheddar cheese,
- 1 bell pepper diced
- 1 can corn drained
- 1 can black beans drained and rinsed
- 1 cup tomatoes, diced
- 2 cups chopped romaine lettuce
- 1 box of jiffy cornbread

Nutrition Facts (per serving):
Calories: 264 kcal,
Proteins:9 g,
Fats: 14.8 g, Carbs: 24.2 g

Directions:

For the Dressing:
1. Place all ingredients for the dressing in your blender, and pulse them until the cilantro is well blended into the avocado and lime juice.

For the Salad:
1. First, prepare the cornbread according to the directions on the box.
2. Once it has cooked through, set it aside and allow it to cool completely.
3. Once it is cooled, cut the cornbread in half and then break half of it up into little crumbs.
4. Put the crumbled cornbread into the bottom of your dish.
5. Using a trifle dish is best because you will be able to see all of the beautiful layers. You can use any bowl that you want if you don't have a trifle dish.
6. Place half of the romaine lettuce on top of the crumbled cornbread. Make sure you evenly spread it across. This is your second layer.
7. Top the lettuce with half of the black beans, ensuring they are evenly distributed.
8. Add half of the corn evenly on top of the beans.
9. Top the corn with half of the chopped bell peppers.
10. Add half of the tomatoes on top of the bell peppers, making sure they are evenly distributed.
11. Sprinkle half of the cheddar cheese on top of the tomatoes.
12. Now drizzle on half of the salad dressing that you made earlier.
13. Repeat this process, starting with the lettuce and through the dressing.
14. To finish the recipe, top everything with green onions and enjoy.
15. You can reserve the rest of the cornbread for another meal or make another salad. The choice is yours.

86. Summer Peach Spinach Salad With Goat's Cheese

Preparation Time: 5 minutes   *Cooking Time: 15 minutes*   *Servings: 6*

Ingredients:

For the Dressing:
- ½ cup toasted almonds
- ½ cup goat cheese crumbles
- ½ a thinly sliced red onion
- 1 diced avocado
- 2 sliced large peaches
- 4 cups of spinach
- 2 tbsp balsamic vinegar

For the Dressing:
- 1 garlic clove minced
- ½ a tsp of Dijon mustard
- 3 tbsp extra virgin olive oil
- 3 tbsp balsamic vinegar
- Salt and pepper

Directions:

1. To make the dressing, combine the Dijon mustard, minced garlic, olive oil, balsamic vinegar, salt, and pepper in a medium-sized bowl and whisk together thoroughly.
2. To make the salad, combine the spinach and the balsamic vinegar, then toss to combine.
3. Add the red onion, goat's cheese, avocado, peach, and toasted almonds and toss to combine.
4. Divide onto plates and serve.

Nutrition Facts (per serving):
Calories: 345 kcal, Proteins: 8.4 g, Fats: 29.6 g, Carbs: 11 g

87. White Chocolate Crumble With Coated Strawberries

Preparation Time: 5 minutes   *Cooking Time: 5 minutes*   *Servings: 4*

Ingredients:

- Mint leaves to serve
- 3 ¼ tbsp chopped pistachios
- 4 tbsp crème fraiche
- 3 ¼ cups strawberries, tops removed, sliced into quarters
- 1 cup melted white chocolate
- ½ cup cornstarch
- ½ cup powdered milk

Nutrition Facts (per serving):
Calories: 348 kcal,
Fats: 15.2 g, Carbs: 44.1 g,
Proteins: 8.7 g

Directions:

1. Prepare the oven by heating it to 300°F.
2. In a large bowl, combine the cornstarch, and milk powder, then toss to combine.
3. Melt the white chocolate in the microwave for 60 seconds and stir to combine.
4. Tip the milk mixture into the white chocolate mixture and stir to combine until a crumble-like texture is achieved.
5. Spread the mixture onto a baking tray and bake until it turns golden in color.
6. Take the tray out of the oven and leave the crumble to cool down.
7. Put the strawberries into a bowl, top with some of the crumble, the pistachios, and a spoonful of créme fraiche.
8. Divide into bowls, top with the mint leaves, and serve.

88. Zucchini Pasta Salad

Preparation Time: 4 minutes   *Cooking Time: 0 minutes*   *Servings: 5*

Ingredients:

- 5 tbsp olive oil
- 2 tsp Dijon mustard
- 3 tbsp red wine vinegar
- 1 garlic clove, grated
- 2 tbsp fresh oregano, chopped
- 1 shallot, chopped
- ¼ tsp red pepper flakes
- 16 oz zucchini noodles
- ¼ cup kalamata olives, pitted
- 3 cups cherry tomatoes, sliced in half
- ¾ cup parmesan cheese, shaved

Directions:

1. Mix the olive oil, dijon mustard, vinegar, garlic, oregano, shallot, and red pepper flakes in a bowl.
2. Stir in the zucchini noodles.
3. Sprinkle on top of the olives, tomatoes, and parmesan cheese.

Nutrition Facts (per serving):
Calories: 250 kcal, Fats: 20 g, Carbs: 10.6 g, Proteins: 7.1 g

CHAPTER 10

Meat and Poultry Recipes

89. Beef Stuffed Zucchini

Preparation Time: 10 minutes   *Cooking Time: 35 minutes*   *Servings: 6*

Ingredients:

For the Stuffing:
- ½ cup long-grain rice rinsed
- ½ lb lean ground beef
- 1 small onion, shredded
- ⅓ cup parsley, chopped
- ⅓ cup dill, chopped
- 1 (14 ½ oz) can diced tomato with juice
- ½ cup water
- 2 tbsp olive oil
- 1 tsp allspice
- 1 tsp garlic powder
- Salt and black pepper, to taste

For the Zucchini:
- 4 large firm tomatoes
- 1 small onion, sliced into circles
- 2 ½ lb medium-sized zucchini, peeled
- 1 (14 ½ oz) can tomato sauce
- ¾ cup water

Directions:

1. Mix the rice with the black pepper, salt, garlic powder, allspice, olive oil, water, diced tomatoes, dill, parsley, onion, and beef in a large bowl.
2. Cut off the tops of 3 tomatoes and remove their cores.
3. Cut off the top of each zucchini and then remove the cores with a corer, leaving the bottom intact.
4. Slice the remaining tomatoes and spread them in a deep, greased pan.
5. Top them with the onion slices and the core of the zucchini.
6. Sprinkle with black pepper and salt.
7. Stuff the tomatoes and cored zucchini with rice stuffing.
8. Place them in the pan, then add water, tomatoes, a sprinkle of black pepper, and salt on top.
9. Place this pan over medium-high heat and cook to a boil.
10. Reduce its heat, cover, and cook for 50 minutes
11. Serve warm.

Nutrition Facts (per serving):
Calories: 233 kcal, Fats: 7.8 g, Carbs: 26.6 g, Proteins: 14.3 g

90. Greek Beef Roast

Preparation Time: 10 minutes   *Cooking Time: 8 hours*   *Servings: 5*

Ingredients:

- 2 lb lean top round beef roast
- 1 tbsp Italian seasoning
- 6 garlic cloves, minced
- 1 onion, sliced
- 2 cups beef broth
- ½ cup red wine
- 1 tsp red pepper flakes
- Pepper
- Salt

Directions:

1. Season the meat with pepper and salt and place into the pot. Pour the remaining ingredients over the meat. Cook on low within 8 hours. Shred the meat using a fork. Serve and enjoy.

Nutrition Facts (per serving):
Calories: 213 kcal, Fats: 4.9 g, Carbs: 0.4 g, Proteins: 38.2 g

91. Lamb Burgers

Preparation Time: 20 minutes   *Cooking Time: 10 minutes*   *Servings: 4*

Ingredients:

- 1 lb ground lamb
- 1 4-inch sprig rosemary, chopped
- 4 sprigs thyme, chopped
- 1 tbsp garlic powder
- 1 pinch salt
- 1 pinch ground black pepper
- 3 tbsp mayonnaise
- 1 tbsp Dijon mustard
- 4 hamburger buns, split and toasted
- 4 thick slices tomato
- 1 cup baby mixed salad green

Directions:

1. Preheat the grill over medium flame. Oil the grate.
2. Combine the pepper, salt, garlic powder, thyme, rosemary, and ground lamb into four patties.
3. Cook the burger for five minutes per side.
4. Combine the mustard and mayonnaise in the bowl.
5. Scatter one tablespoon of the mixture on the sides of each bun.
6. Place the burger onto each bun and top with greens and tomato.
7. Variation tip, you can add beef and lamb.
8. Serving suggestion, sprinkle with feta cheese.
9. Serve in a pita or bun.

Nutrition Facts (per serving):
Calories:455 kcal, Fats: 12.1 g, Carbs: 69.5 g, Proteins: 17.2 g

92. Grilled Steak, Mushroom, and Onion Kebabs

Preparation Time: 15 minutes   *Cooking Time: 15 minutes*   *Servings: 4*

Ingredients:

- Non-stick cooking spray.
- 4 garlic cloves, peeled.
- 2 fresh rosemary sprigs (about 3 inches each).
- 2 tbsp extra-virgin olive oil, divided.
- 1 pound boneless top sirloin steak, about 1 inch thick 1 (8 oz) package white button mushrooms.
- 1 medium red onion, cut into 12 thin wedges.
- ¼ tsp coarsely ground black pepper.
- 2 tbsp red wine vinegar.
- ¼ tsp kosher or sea salt.

Directions:

1. Soak 12 (10-inch) wooden skewers in water. Spray the cold grill with non-stick cooking spray, and heat the grill to medium-high.
2. Cut a piece of aluminum foil into a 10-inch square. Place the garlic and rosemary sprigs in the center, drizzle with one oil tablespoon, and wrap tightly to form a foil packet. Place it on the grill, and close the grill cover.
3. Cut the steak into 1-inch cubes. Thread the beef onto the wet skewers, alternating with whole mushrooms and onion wedges. Spray the kebabs thoroughly with non-stick cooking spray, and sprinkle with pepper.
4. Cook the kebabs on the covered grill for 4 to 5 minutes. Turn and grill for 4 to 5 more minutes, covered, until a meat thermometer inserted in the meat registers 145°F (medium rare) or 160°F (medium).
5. Remove the foil packet from the grill, open it, and, using tongs, place the garlic and rosemary sprigs in a small bowl. Carefully strip the rosemary sprigs of their leaves into the bowl and pour in any accumulated juices and oil from the foil packet. Add the remaining oil tablespoon, vinegar, and salt. Mash the garlic with a fork, and mix all ingredients in the bowl together. Pour over the finished steak kebabs and serve.

Nutrition Facts (per serving):
Calories: 270 kcal, Fats: 18.1 g, Carbs: 2.6 g, Proteins: 24.4 g

Preparation Time: 15 minutes   *Cooking Time: 10 minutes*   *Servings: 4*

Ingredients:

- Non-stick cooking spray.
- 2 tbsp extra-virgin olive oil.
- 1 tbsp dried oregano.
- 1 ¼ tsp garlic powder, divided.
- 1 tsp ground cumin.
- ½ tsp freshly ground black pepper.
- ¼ tsp kosher or sea salt.
- 1 pound beef flank steak, top round steak, or lamb leg steak, center cut, about 1 inch thick.
- 1 medium green bell pepper, halved and seeded.
- 2 tbsp tahini or peanut butter.
- 1 tbsp hot water.
- ½ cup 2% plain Greek yogurt.
- 1 tbsp freshly squeezed lemon juice (about ½ small lemon).
- 1 cup thinly sliced red onion (about ½ onion).
- 4 (6-inch) whole-wheat pita bread, warmed.

Directions:

1. Set an oven rack about 4 inches below the broiler. Preheat the oven broiler to high. Line a large, rimmed baking sheet with foil. Place a wire cooling rack on the foil, and spray the rack with non-stick cooking spray. Set aside.
2. Whisk the oil, oregano, and 1 teaspoon of garlic powder, cumin, pepper, and salt in a small bowl. Rub the oil mixture on all sides of the steak, saving one teaspoon of the mixture.
3. Place the steak on the prepared rack. Rub the remaining oil mixture on the bell pepper, place it on the rack, and cut the side down. Press the pepper with the heel of your hand to flatten it.
4. Broil for 5 minutes. Turn the meat and the pepper pieces, and broil for 2 to 5 more minutes until the pepper is charred and the internal temperature of the meat measures 145°F on a meat thermometer. Put the pepper and steak on a cutting board to rest for 5 minutes.
5. While the meat is broiling, in a small bowl, whisk the tahini until smooth (adding one tablespoon of hot water if your tahini is sticky). Add the remaining garlic powder, yogurt, and lemon juice, then whisk thoroughly.
6. Slice the steak crosswise into ¼-inch-thick strips. Slice the bell pepper into strips. Divide the steak, bell pepper, and onion among the warm pita bread. Drizzle with tahini sauce and serve.

Nutrition Facts (per serving):
Calories: 415 kcal, Fats: 13.6 g, Carbs: 39.3 g, Proteins: 33.9 g

94. Ground Beef Skillet

Preparation Time: 15 minutes   *Cooking Time: 70 minutes*   *Servings: 6*

Ingredients:

- 1 spaghetti squash
- 2 tsp olive oil
- Salt, black pepper, and garlic powder to taste
- 1 lb lean ground beef
- 1 small onion, diced
- 1 bell pepper, diced
- 3 garlic cloves, minced
- 1 cup baby Bella mushrooms, chopped
- 2 (15 oz) canned diced tomatoes
- 1 (15 oz) can of tomato sauce
- 1 tbsp Italian seasoning
- Salt and black pepper to taste
- ¼ cup basil, chopped
- 2 tbsp parmesan cheese

Directions:

1. Preheat your oven to 400°F.
2. Cut the prepared squash in half; lengthwise, remove the seed and rub it with garlic powder, black pepper, salt, and olive oil.
3. Place the cut squash with the skin side down on a baking sheet and roast for 40 minutes in the preheated oven.
4. Scrap out the roasted squash with a fork and transfer it to a plate.
5. Sauté the beef in a skillet until brown.
6. Stir in pepper and onion, then sauté for 5 minutes
7. Add garlic, mushrooms, black pepper, and salt, then sauté for 5 minutes
8. Stir in Italian seasoning, tomato sauce, and diced tomatoes.
9. Cook for 20 minutes, then garnish with parsley.
10. Serve the beef on top of the spaghetti squash.
11. Enjoy.
12. Serving suggestion; serve the beef with sautéed carrots on the side.
13. Variation tip; drizzle parmesan cheese on top before serving.

Nutrition Facts (per serving):
Calories: 306 kcal, Fats: 13.9 g, Carbs: 8.2 g, Proteins: 36.9 g

Preparation Time: 20 minutes   *Cooking Time: 15 minutes*   *Servings: 15*

Ingredients:

- 5 lb boneless lamb shoulder cut into 1-inch pieces
- 6 tbsp Dijon mustard
- 4 tbsp white wine vinegar
- 4 tbsp olive oil
- ½ tsp salt
- ½ tsp black pepper
- ½ tsp fresh rosemary chopped
- ½ tsp crumbled dried sage
- 4 garlic cloves chopped
- 4 green bell peppers cut into large chunks
- 10 oz whole fresh mushrooms
- 16 oz pineapple chunks drained with juice reserved
- 1-pint cherry tomatoes
- 4 onions, quartered
- 10 oz maraschino cherries, drained and juice reserved
- ⅓ cup melted butter or margarine

Directions:

1. Add the lamb to the bowl.
2. Add garlic, sage, rosemary, pepper, salt, olive oil, vinegar, and mustard in another bowl.
3. Add over the lamb and combine well to coat.
4. Cover with a lid and place into the refrigerator overnight.
5. Preheat the grill over a high flame.
6. Place the vegetables, fruits, and marinated lamb on bamboo skewers.
7. Reserve the juice from cherries and pineapple.
8. Add melted butter and the juice from pineapple and cherries into the bowl to make a basting sauce.
9. Place on the preheated grill and cook for twelve minutes
10. Brush with butter sauce during grilling.
11. Variation tip; you can add margarine instead of butter.
12. Serving Suggestion; serve with yogurt and warm pita.

Nutrition Facts (per serving):
Calories: 426 kcal, Fats: 20.3 g, Carbs: 23.6 g, Proteins: 36.5 g

96. Lemon Chicken Skewers

Preparation Time: 10 minutes   *Cooking Time: 16 minutes*   *Servings: 4*

Ingredients:

- ¼ cup olive oil
- 3 tbsp lemon juice
- 1 tbsp white wine vinegar
- 2 garlic cloves, minced
- 3 tsp grated lemon zest
- 2 tsp salt
- ½ tsp sugar
- ¼ tsp dried oregano
- ¼ tsp pepper
- 1- ½ lb chicken breasts, boneless, skinless, and cut into 1- ½ -inch pieces
- 3 zucchinis, halved lengthwise and sliced into 1- ½ -inch pieces
- 2 onions, cut into wedges
- 12 cherry tomatoes

Directions:

1. Mix the olive oil, lemon juice, white wine vinegar, garlic cloves, lemon zest, salt, sugar, dried oregano, and pepper in a bowl. Keep it aside. Reserve ¼ cup for basting.
2. Add half of the mixture into the big bowl, then add the chicken and coat well.
3. Add the remaining marinade to another bowl. Add the tomatoes, onion, and zucchini, then coat well.
4. Cover with a lid and place it into the fridge for up to 4 hours.
5. Remove the marinade and drain it.
6. Thread the vegetables and chicken onto the soaked skewers. Place them on the grill and cook for six minutes per side—occasionally baste with the reserved marinade.
7. Serving Suggestion, top with sliced lemon, mint, and red onion.
8. Serve with pickled cabbage and chili sauce.

Nutrition Facts (per serving):
Calories: 247 kcal, Fats: 11.6 g, Carbs: 5.1 g, Proteins: 30.7 g

CHAPTER 11

Soups Recipes

97. Creamy Tomato Soup

Preparation Time: 45 minutes　　　*Cooking Time: 6 minutes*　　　*Servings: 4*

Ingredients:

- 1 lb fresh tomatoes, halved
- 15 oz can tomatoes
- 2 red bell peppers, sliced
- 1 tbsp olive oil
- 2 cups Vegetable stock
- pepper
- salt

Directions:

1. Preheat the oven to 400°F/ 200°C
2. Place the tomatoes and bell peppers on a baking tray and drizzle with oil.
3. Roast in preheated oven for 20 minutes
4. Transfer the roasted tomatoes and peppers to a saucepan along with the remaining ingredients and cook over medium heat for 15-20 minutes.
5. Puree the soup using a blender until smooth and creamy.
6. Season with pepper and salt.
7. Serve and enjoy.

Nutrition Facts (per serving):

Calories: 147 kcal, Fats: 5.1 g, Carbs: 19.2 g, Proteins: 6.2 g

98. Beef, Mushroom, and Barley Soup

Preparation Time: 5 minutes   *Cooking Time: 60 minutes*   *Servings: 4*

Ingredients:

- 1 lb beef cubes, cut from a chuck roast.
- ¼ red onion, chopped
- 2 garlic cloves, crushed
- 1 15 oz can mushroom, drained
- 2 cups homemade beef broth
- 2 ½ cups water
- ½ cup pearled barley
- Salt and pepper to taste
- Fresh parsley to garnish (optional)
- Homemade bread from the freezer
- 15 oz can corn

Directions:

1. In a large pan, brown the beef cubes on all sides with the chopped onion and crushed garlic.
2. Add the drained mushrooms, homemade beef broth, and water to the pan.
3. Bring the liquid to a boil, then add the pearled barley.
4. Reduce the heat to a simmer and let cook for 20 minutes, until the barley is tender.
5. Season with salt and pepper to taste.
6. Toast the homemade bread and cut it into slices.
7. Heat the canned corn in a separate pot or in the microwave.
8. Serve the beef and barley soup with the toasted bread and corn on the side.
9. Garnish with fresh parsley if desired.

Nutrition Facts (per serving):
Calories: 279 kcal, Carbs: 47.3 g, Fats: 2.5 g, Proteins: 16.9 g

99. Cauliflower and Sweet Corn Bisque

Preparation Time: 5 minutes *Cooking Time: 50 minutes* *Servings: 5*

Ingredients:

- 2 to 3 tbsp extra-virgin olive oil
- 1 large onion, chopped
- 1 small-medium-sized head of cauliflower, chopped
- 2 garlic cloves, chopped
- 2 ears sweet corn
- Salt to taste
- White pepper to taste
- A pinch cayenne pepper
- 1 tbsp olive oil
- Fresh thyme or other fresh herbs for garnish
- Water

Directions:

1. Heat the extra-virgin olive oil in a deep-bottomed pot over low heat. Add the chopped onions and a pinch of salt. Cook for 5 minutes, occasionally stirring, until translucent.
2. Add the chopped cauliflower and garlic to the pot. Increase the heat to medium and add another pinch of salt, white pepper, and a pinch of cayenne pepper. Cook for about 5 minutes, stirring occasionally, until the cauliflower is lightly browned and tender.
3. Shuck the corn and cut off the kernels. Reserve half of the kernels and add the other half and corn cobs to the pot. Add enough water to cover the corn cobs and bring to a boil, stirring occasionally. Reduce the heat to a simmer and let cook for 30 minutes.
4. Remove the corn cobs from the soup. Use a hand blender to puree the soup until smooth. Add the reserved corn kernels to the soup and cook for a few minutes to warm through. Add salt and white pepper to taste, and mix in the optional butter.
5. If desired, serve hot, garnished with fresh thyme or other fresh herbs.

Nutrition Facts (per serving):
Calories: 206 kcal, Fats: 11.2 g, Carbs: 20.1 g, Proteins: 6.2 g

100. Cheesy Mushroom Soup

Ingredients:

- 2 tbsp olive oil
- 4 oz fresh baby portobello mushroom, sliced
- 4 oz fresh white button mushrooms, sliced
- ½ cup yellow onion, chopped
- ½ tsp salt
- 2 tsp garlic, chopped
- 3 cups low-sodium vegetable broth
- 1 cup low-fat cheddar cheese

Directions:

1. Heat the oil over medium heat in a medium pan and cook the mushrooms and onion with salt for about 5-7 minutes, stirring frequently.
2. Add the garlic, and sauté for about 1-2 minutes
3. Stir in the broth and remove from the heat.
4. With a stick blender, blend the soup until the mushrooms are chopped very finely.
5. Add the cheddar cheese to the pan, and stir to combine.
6. Place the pan over medium heat and cook for about 3-5 minutes
7. Remove from the heat and serve immediately.

Nutrition Facts (per serving):
Calories: 186 kcal, Fats: 15.3 g, Carbs: 2.4 g, Proteins: 9.8 g

101. Pepper Salmon Skewers

Ingredients:

- 1.5 lb salmon fillet
- ½ cup Plain yogurt
- 1 tsp paprika
- 1 tsp turmeric
- 1 tsp red pepper
- 1 tsp salt
- 1 tsp dried cilantro
- 1 tsp sunflower oil
- ½ tsp ground nutmeg

Directions:

1. Mix up together Plain yogurt, paprika, turmeric, red pepper, salt, and ground nutmeg for the marinade.
2. Chop the salmon fillet roughly and put it in the yogurt mixture.
3. Mix up well and marinate for 25 minutes
4. Then skew the fish on the skewers.
5. Sprinkle the skewers with sunflower oil and place them in the tray.
6. Bake the salmon skewers for 15 minutes at 375°F.

Nutrition Facts (per serving):
Calories: 254 kcal, Fats: 20.5 g, Carbs: 3 g, Protein: 27.4 g

Preparation Time: 15 minutes *Cooking Time: 30 minutes* *Servings: 4*

Ingredients:

- 2 tbsp olive oil
- 2 onions, chopped
- 3 garlic cloves, minced
- ½ pound fresh button mushrooms, chopped
- ¼ pound fresh shiitake mushrooms, chopped
- ¼ pound fresh spinach, chopped
- Sea salt and freshly ground black pepper, as required
- ¼ cup low-sodium vegetable broth
- ½ cup coconut milk
- 2 tbsp fresh parsley, chopped

Directions:

1. Heat oil over medium heat in a large wok and sauté the onion and garlic for 4-5 minutes.
2. Add the mushrooms, salt, and black pepper and cook for 4-5 minutes
3. Bring the spinach, broth, and coconut milk to a gentle boil.
4. Simmer for 4-5 minutes or until the desired doneness.
5. Stir in the parsley and remove from the heat.
6. Serve hot.

Nutrition Facts (per serving):
Calories: 242 kcal, Fats: 15.6 g, Carbs: 12.2 g, Proteins: 13 g

103. Tofu & Mushroom Soup

Preparation Time: 15 minutes   *Cooking Time: 25 minutes*   *Servings: 6*

Ingredients:

- 3 tbsp vegetable oil, divided
- 1 shallot, minced
- 1 oz fresh ginger, minced
- 2 garlic cloves, minced
- 5 ½ oz coconut milk
- 1 Roma tomato, chopped
- 1 lemongrass stalk, halved crosswise
- 6 oz fresh mushrooms, sliced
- 14 oz extra-firm tofu, pressed, drained, and cut into ½-inch cubes
- Ground black pepper, as required
- 1 scallion, sliced
- 1 tbsp fresh cilantro, chopped
- Salt
- Water

Directions:

1. Heat 2 tablespoons of oil over medium-high heat in a pan and sauté the shallot, ginger, garlic, and a pinch of salt for about 1-2 minutes.
2. Add coconut milk and the remaining water, then bring to a boil.
3. Add the tomato and lemongrass, then stir to combine.
4. Adjust the heat to low and simmer for about 8-10 minutes
5. Meanwhile, in a large non-stick wok, heat the remaining oil over medium-high heat and cook the mushrooms, tofu, pinch of salt, and black pepper for about 5-8 minutes, stirring occasionally.
6. Remove the lemongrass stalk from the pan of soup and discard it.
7. Divide the cooked mushrooms and tofu into serving bowls evenly.
8. Top with hot soup and serve with the garnishing of scallion and cilantro.

Nutrition Facts (per serving):
Calories: 219 kcal, Fats: 6.8 g, Carbs: 20 g, Proteins: 19.5 g

104. Filling Macaroni Soup

Preparation Time: 10 minutes   *Cooking Time: 45 minutes*   *Servings: 6*

Ingredients:

- 1 cup minced beef or chicken or a combination of both
- 1 cup carrots, diced
- 1 cup milk
- ½ medium onion, sliced thinly
- 3 garlic cloves, minced
- Salt and pepper to taste
- 2 cups broth (chicken, vegetable, or beef)
- ½ tbsp olive oil
- 1 cup uncooked whole wheat pasta like macaroni, shells, or even angel hair broken to pieces
- 1 cup water

Directions:

1. In a heavy-bottomed pot on medium-high fire, heat oil.
2. Add the garlic and sauté for a minute or two until fragrant but not browned.
3. Add the onions and sauté for 3 minutes or until soft and translucent.
4. Add a cup of minced meat. You can also use whatever leftover frozen meat you have.
5. Sauté the meat well until cooked, around 8 minutes. While sautéing, season the meat with pepper and salt.
6. Add water and broth and bring to a boil.
7. Once boiling, add pasta. I use any leftover pasta that I have in the pantry. If all you have left is spaghetti, lasagna, angel hair, or fettuccine, just break them into pieces—around 1 inch in length before adding them to the pot.
8. Slow fire to a simmer and cook while covered until the pasta is soft.
9. Add the carrots halfway through cooking the pasta, around 8 minutes.
10. Once the pasta is soft, turn off the fire and add milk.
11. Mix well and season to taste again if needed.
12. Serve and enjoy.

Nutrition Facts (per serving):
Calories: 213 kcal, Carbs: 27.9 g; Proteins: 13.6g, Fats: 5.3 g

105. Zucchini Soup

⁂ Preparation Time: 20 minutes   *🍲 Cooking Time: 20 minutes*   *🍽 Servings:4*

🥣 Ingredients:

- 2 ½ lb zucchini, peeled and sliced
- ⅓ cup basil leaves
- 4 cups vegetable stock
- 4 garlic cloves, chopped
- 2 tbsp olive oil
- 1 medium onion, diced
- Pepper, to taste
- Salt, to taste

⌧ Directions:

1. Heat olive oil at a low temperature in a pan.
2. Add the onion and zucchini, then sauté until tender for one minute; add the garlic and sauté again.
3. Add the vegetable stock and boil for 15 minutes.
4. Remove from the heat; basil should be added after the soup has been blended to a smooth and creamy consistency. Add salt and pepper to taste.
5. Stir thoroughly, then plate.

Nutrition Facts (per serving):
Calories: 138 kcal, Fats: 8.9 g, Carbs: 9 g, Proteins: 5.6 g

CHAPTER 12

Fish and Seafood Recipes

106. Baked Halibut Steaks

Preparation Time: 10 minutes   *Cooking Time: 20 minutes*   *Servings: 4*

Ingredients:
- 1 tsp olive oil
- 1 cup zucchini, diced
- ½ cup onion, minced
- 1 garlic clove, peeled and minced
- 2 cups fresh tomatoes, diced
- 2 tbsp fresh basil, chopped
- ¼ tsp salt
- ¼ tsp black pepper
- 4 (6 oz) halibut steaks
- ⅓ cup feta cheese, crumbled

Directions:
1. Preheat your oven to 450°F.
2. Grease a shallow baking dish with cooking oil.
3. Sauté the onion, garlic, and zucchini for 5 minutes
4. Stir in the tomatoes, black pepper, salt, and basil.
5. Mix well and remove this mixture from the heat.
6. Place the halibut steaks in the prepared baking dish.
7. Top the steaks with the zucchini mixture and feta cheese.
8. Bake the fish for 15 minutes in the oven.
9. Serve warm.

Nutrition Facts (per serving):
Calories: 279 kcal, Fats: 15.4 g, Carbs: 3.7 g, Proteins: 31.2 g

107. Branzino Mediterranean

Preparation Time: 10 minutes   *Cooking Time: 30 minutes*   *Servings: 2*

Ingredients:

- 2 tbsp olive oil
- 3 sprigs fresh rosemary
- 1 white onion, chopped
- 1 tbsp fresh oregano leaves
- 3 wedges fresh lemon
- ½ cup white wine
- ⅓ cup lemon juice
- 2 whole Branzino (sea bass) fish, cleaned
- ¼ cup Italian parsley, chopped
- Black pepper and salt to taste

Directions:

1. Preheat your oven to 300°F.
2. Toss the onion in a baking pan with one1 tablespoon of olive oil, black pepper, and salt.
3. Place the fish in the pan and stuff it with some red onion, one rosemary sprig, and one lemon wedge.
4. Pour the lemon juice, white wine, and oregano on top.
5. Drizzle one tablespoon of oil on top of the fish.
6. Bake the fish for 30 minutes in the oven.
7. Once it is done, remove the bones from the fish.
8. Garnish with lemon wedges and parsley.
9. Serve warm.

Nutrition Facts (per serving):
Calories: 372 kcal, Fats: 16.2 g, Carbs: 5.3 g, Proteins: 43.8 g

108. Grilled Lemon Pesto Salmon

Preparation Time: 5 minutes   *Cooking Time: 10 minutes*   *Servings: 2*

Ingredients:

- 10 oz (283 g) salmon fillet
- 2 tbsp prepared pesto sauce
- 1 large fresh lemon, sliced
- Cooking spray

Directions:

1. Preheat a grill to medium-high heat. Spray the grill grates with cooking spray.
2. Season the salmon well. Spread the pesto sauce on top.
3. Make a bed of fresh lemon slices about the same size as the salmon fillet on the hot grill, and place the salmon on top of the lemon slices. Put any additional lemon slices on top of the salmon.
4. Grill the salmon for 10 minutes.
5. Serve hot.

Nutrition Facts (per serving):
Calories: 391 kcal, Fats: 28.7 g, Proteins: 27.5 g, Carbs: 5.7 g

Preparation Time: 10 minutes   *Cooking Time: 40 minutes*   *Servings: 4*

Ingredients:

- 5 Roma tomatoes, diced
- 2 tbsp olive oil
- ½ Spanish onion, chopped
- 2 garlic cloves, chopped
- 1 pinch Italian seasoning
- 24 Kalamata olives, pitted and chopped
- ¼ cup white wine
- ¼ cup capers
- 1 tsp fresh lemon juice
- 6 leaves fresh basil, chopped
- 3 tbsp parmesan cheese, grated
- 1 lb flounder fillets
- Water

Directions:

1. Preheat your oven to 425°F.
2. Boil water in a pan and dip the tomatoes in it for 1 minute.
3. Transfer the tomatoes to an ice bath, allow them to cool, then remove the skins.
4. Remove the seeds, then chop up the tomatoes.
5. Sauté the onion with oil in a skillet for 5 minutes
6. Stir in the garlic, Italian seasoning, and tomatoes, then sauté for 7 minutes
7. Add ½ the basil along with the lemon juice, capers, wine, and olives, then reduce the heat.
8. Stir in the Parmesan cheese and cook for 15 minutes, stirring occasionally., stirring occasionally.
9. Place the flounder fish onto a shallow baking dish, and pour the sauce on top of it.
10. Add the remaining basil leaves on top and bake for twelve minutes.
11. Serve warm.

Nutrition Facts (per serving):
Calories: 242 kcal, Fats: 14.2 g, Carbs: 3.8 g, Proteins: 22.4 g

110. Grilled Mediterranean Salmon

Preparation Time: 10 minutes   *Cooking Time: 8 minutes*   *Servings: 4*

Ingredients:

- 1 (10 oz) basket cherry tomatoes, quartered
- 4 tbsp olive oil
- 1 small shallot, chopped
- 2 tbsp black olive tapenade
- ½ tsp salt
- 8 basil leaves
- 4 small fresh thyme sprigs
- Black pepper, to taste
- 4 (12x18-inch) pieces aluminum foil
- 4 (7 oz) salmon filets with skin

Directions:

1. At high heat, preheat your grill and grease its grates.
2. Toss the cherry tomatoes with the black pepper, thyme, basil salt, tapenade, shallots, and olive oil in a bowl.
3. Spread a sheet of foil on a working surface.
4. Place the salmon on the foil sheet and top it with ¼ of the cherry tomato mixture and fold the edges of the foil.
5. Place the salmon packets on the grill, cover the hood, and cook for eight minutes.
6. Serve warm.

Nutrition Facts (per serving):
Calories: 556 kcal, Fats: 41.7 g, Carbs: 6.6 g, Proteins: 38.5 g

111. Mackerel and Orange Medley

Preparation Time: 10 minutes   *Cooking Time: 10 minutes*   *Servings: 4*

Ingredients:

- 4 mackerel fillets, skinless and boneless
- 4 spring onions, chopped
- 1 tsp olive oil
- 1-inch piece ginger, grated
- Black pepper as needed
- Juice and zest 1 whole orange
- 1 cup low-sodium fish stock

Directions:

1. Season the fillets with black pepper and rub olive oil.
2. Add stock, orange juice, ginger, orange zest, and onion to an Instant Pot.
3. Place a steamer basket and add the fillets.
4. Lock the lid and cook on HIGH pressure for 10 minutes
5. Release the pressure naturally over 10 minutes
6. Divide the fillets among plates and drizzle the orange sauce from the pot over the fish.
7. Enjoy!

Nutrition Facts (per serving):
Calories: 305 kcal, Fats: 18 g, Carbs: 12.6 g, Proteins: 22.9 g

112. Salmon With Peas and Parsley Dressing

Preparation Time: 15 minutes   *Cooking Time: 15 minutes*   *Servings: 2*

Ingredients:

- 16 oz salmon fillets, boneless and skin-on
- 1 tbsp parsley, chopped
- 10 oz peas
- 9 oz vegetable stock, low sodium
- 2 cups water
- ½ tsp oregano, dried
- ½ tsp sweet paprika
- 2 garlic cloves, minced
- A pinch black pepper

Directions:

1. Add garlic, parsley, paprika, oregano, and stock to a food processor and blend.
2. Add water to your Instant Pot.
3. Add a steam basket.
4. Add fish fillets inside the steamer basket.
5. Season with pepper.
6. Lock the lid and cook on HIGH pressure for 10 minutes
7. Release the pressure naturally over 10 minutes.
8. Divide the fish amongst plates.
9. Add peas to the steamer basket and lock the lid again; cook on HIGH pressure for five minutes.
10. Quickly release the pressure.
11. Divide the peas next to your fillets and serve with the parsley dressing drizzled on top
12. Enjoy!

Nutrition Facts (per serving):
Calories: 272 kcal, Fats: 14 g, Carbs: 10.6 g, Proteins: 26.1 g

113. Whitefish in Tomato-Fennel Broth

Preparation Time: 10 minutes   *Cooking Time: 25 minutes*   *Servings: 1*

Ingredients:

- 1 tbsp olive oil
- 2 bulbs fennel, chopped
- 1 onion, chopped
- 1 ½ lb whitefish fillets
- 1 pinch of saffron
- 1 tbsp fennel seeds
- 1 cup diced tomatoes
- 1 cup water

Directions:

1. Sauté the fennel bulbs, onion, and oil in a skillet for 5 minutes
2. Stir in the water, tomatoes, fennel seeds, saffron, and whitefish.
3. Cook the fish to a boil, cover, and leave for 10 minutes
4. Serve warm.

Nutrition Facts (per serving):
Calories: 252 kcal, Fats: 15.8 g, Carbs: 19.59 g, Proteins: 7.4 g

114. Shrimp Fra Diavolo

Preparation Time: 10 minutes　　　*Cooking Time: 28 minutes*　　　*Servings: 4*

Ingredients:

- 1 lb large shrimp, peeled and deveined
- 2 tbsp olive oil
- 1 tsp red pepper flakes
- 1 tsp salt
- 1 pinch Aleppo pepper flakes
- ½ yellow onion, sliced
- 3 garlic cloves, minced
- ½ tsp dried oregano
- 1 cup white wine
- 1 ½ cup canned crushed tomatoes
- 2 tbsp fresh parsley, chopped
- 2 tbsp fresh basil, sliced leaves

Directions:

1. Mix the shrimp with the Aleppo pepper flakes, salt, red pepper flakes, and olive oil in a bowl.
2. Place a large skillet over high heat.
3. Sauté the shrimp for four minutes, then transfer it into a bowl.
4. Sauté the onion in the same skillet with a pinch of salt for four minutes
5. Stir in the oregano and garlic, then sauté for 30 seconds.
6. Pour in the white wine and bring it to a boil.
7. Add the crushed tomatoes, then reduce the heat to medium-low.
8. Cook for 15 minutes, stirring occasionally.
9. Put the sautéed shrimp back into the skillet and cook for four minutes
10. Garnish with the Aleppo pepper flakes, red pepper flakes, salt, basil, and parsley.
11. Enjoy.

Nutrition Facts (per serving):
Calories: 297 kcal, Fats: 9.1 g, Carbs: 10 g, Proteins: 34.8 g

115. Simple One Pot Mussels

Preparation Time: 10 minutes   *Cooking Time: 5 minutes*   *Servings: 4*

Ingredients:
- 2 tbsp butter
- 2 chopped shallots
- 4 garlic cloves minced
- ½ cup broth
- ½ cup white wine
- 2 lb cleaned mussels
- Lemon and parsley for serving

Directions:
1. Clean the mussels and remove the beard.
2. Discard any mussels that do not close when tapped against a hard surface.
3. Set your pot to Sauté mode and add chopped onion and butter.
4. Stir and sauté onions.
5. Add garlic and cook for one minute.
6. Add broth and wine.
7. Lock the lid and cook for five minutes on HIGH pressure.
8. Release the pressure naturally over 10 minutes
9. Serve with a sprinkle of parsley, and enjoy!

Nutrition Facts (per serving):
Calories: 273 kcal, Fats: 12.4 g, Carbs: 9 g, Proteins: 26.8 g

116. Spiced Up Salmon

Preparation Time: 10 minutes   *Cooking Time: 5 minutes*   *Servings: 4*

Ingredients:
- 4 salmon fillets
- 2 tbsp olive oil
- 1 tsp cumin, ground
- 1 tsp sweet paprika
- 1 tsp chili powder
- ½ tsp garlic powder
- A pinch pepper

Directions:
1. Add cumin, paprika, onion, chili powder, garlic powder, and pepper, then toss well in a bowl.
2. Rub the salmon in the mixture.
3. Place a pan over medium heat; add oil and let it heat up.
4. Add the salmon and cook for five minutes on both sides.
5. Divide between plates and serve.
6. Enjoy!

Nutrition Facts (per serving):
Calories: 366 kcal, Fats: 26 g, Carbs: 4.8 g, Proteins: 28.4 g

117. Spicy Chili Salmon

Preparation Time: 15 minutes   *Cooking Time: 7 minutes*   *Servings: 4*

Ingredients:
- 4 salmon fillets, boneless and skin-on
- 2 tbsp assorted chili peppers, chopped
- Juice 1 lemon
- 1 lemon, sliced
- 1 cup water
- Black pepper

Directions:
1. Add water to the Instant Pot.
2. Add the steamer basket and add the salmon fillets, and season them with salt and pepper.
3. Drizzle lemon juice on top.
4. Top with lemon slices.
5. Lock the lid and cook on HIGH pressure for 7 minutes.
6. Release the pressure naturally over 10 minutes
7. Divide the salmon and lemon slices between serving plates.
8. Enjoy!

Nutrition Facts (per serving):
Calories: 378 kcal, Fats: 24 g, Carbs: 3.1 g, Proteins: 37.2 g

118. Steamed Trout With Lemon Herb Crust

Preparation Time: 10 minutes   *Cooking Time:15 minutes*   *Servings: 2*

Ingredients:
- 3 tbsp olive oil
- 3 garlic cloves, chopped
- 2 tbsp fresh lemon juice
- 1 tbsp chopped fresh mint
- 1 tbsp chopped fresh parsley
- ¼ tsp dried ground thyme
- 1 tsp sea salt
- 1 pound (454 g) fresh trout (2 pieces)
- 2 cups fish stock

Directions:
1. Blend olive oil, garlic, lemon juice, mint, parsley, thyme, and salt. Brush the marinade onto the fish.
2. Insert a trivet in the Instant Pot. Fill in the fish stock and place the fish on the trivet.
3. Secure the lid. Select the Steam mode and set the cooking time for 15 minutes at High Pressure.
4. Once cooking is complete, do a quick pressure release. Carefully open the lid. Serve warm.

Nutrition Facts (per serving):
Calories: 417 kcal, Fats: 30.3 g, Proteins: 34.6 g, Carbs: 1.7 g

CHAPTER 13
Vegetarian Dishes Recipes

119. Broccoli and Cauliflower Mash

Preparation Time: 2 minutes   *Cooking Time: 13 minutes*   *Servings: 2*

Ingredients:

- ½ Lb (227 g) broccoli florets
- ½ lb (227 g) cauliflower florets
- ½ tsp garlic powder
- 1 tsp shallot powder
- 4 tbsp whipped cheese
- 1 ½ tbsp olive oil

Directions:

1. Microwave the broccoli and cauliflower for about 13 minutes until they have softened completely. Transfer to a food processor and add in the remaining ingredients.
2. Process until everything is well combined.
3. Taste and adjust the seasoning. Bon appétit!

Nutrition Facts (per serving):
Calories: 267 kcal, Fats: 20.8 g, Proteins: 11.4 g, Carbs: 8.7 g

120. Cheesy Cauliflower Falafel

Preparation Time: 20 minutes   *Cooking Time: 15 minutes*   *Servings: 2*

Ingredients:

- 1 head cauliflower, cut into florets
- ⅓ cup silvered ground almonds
- Cheddar cheese, shredded
- ½ tsp mixed spice
- Salt and chili pepper to taste
- Coconut flour
- 4 Fresh eggs
- Ghee

Directions:

1. Blend the florets in a blender until a grain meal consistency is formed.
2. Pour the rice into a bowl, and add the ground almonds, mixed spice, salt, cheddar cheese, chili pepper, and coconut flour until evenly combined.
3. Beat the eggs until creamy in color and mix with the cauliflower mixture.
4. Shape ¼ cup each into patties.
5. Melt ghee and fry the patties for 5 minutes on each side until firm and browned.
6. Remove onto a wire rack to cool, share into serving plates, and top with tahini sauce.

Nutrition Facts (per serving):
Calories: 235 kcal, Fats: 18.6 g, Carbs: 4.4 g, Proteins: 10 g

121. Eggplant Pizza With Tofu

Preparation Time: 15 minutes   *Cooking Time: 45 minutes*   *Servings: 4*

Ingredients:

- 2 eggplants, sliced
- 2 tsp olive oil
- 2 garlic cloves, minced
- Red onion
- 12 oz tofu, chopped
- Tomato sauce
- Salt and black pepper to taste
- ½ tsp Cinnamon powder
- 1 cup parmesan cheese, shredded
- ¼ cup dried oregano

Directions:

1. Let the oven heat to 400°F. Lay the eggplant slices on a baking sheet and brush with some olive oil. Bake in the oven until lightly browned, about twenty minutes.
2. Sauté garlic and onion until fragrant and soft, about 3 minutes
3. Stir in the tofu and cook for 3 minutes. Add the tomato sauce, salt, and black pepper. Simmer for 10 minutes
4. Sprinkle with parmesan cheese and oregano. Bake for 10 minutes.

Nutrition Facts (per serving):
Calories: 259 kcal, Fats: 18.7 g, Carbs: 5.5 g, Proteins: 16.8 g

122. Eggplant Ratatouille

Preparation Time: 15 minutes   *Cooking Time: 15 minutes*   *Servings: 2*

Ingredients:

- 1 eggplant
- 1 sweet yellow pepper
- 3 cherry tomatoes
- ⅓ white onion, chopped
- ½ tsp garlic clove, sliced
- 1 tsp olive oil
- ½ tsp ground black pepper
- ½ tsp Italian seasoning

Directions:

1. Preheat the air fryer to 360°F.
2. Peel the eggplants and chop them.
3. Put the chopped eggplants in the air fryer basket.
4. Chop the cherry tomatoes and add them to the air fryer basket.
5. Then add the chopped onion, sliced garlic clove, olive oil, ground black pepper, and Italian seasoning.
6. Chop the sweet yellow pepper roughly and add it to the air fryer basket.
7. Shake the vegetables gently and cook for 15 minutes.
8. Stir the meal after 8 minutes of cooking.
9. Transfer the cooked ratatouille to the serving plates.
10. Enjoy!

Nutrition Facts (per serving):
Calories: 155 kcal, Fats: 8.4 g, Carbs: 16.1 g, Proteins: 3.8 g

Preparation Time: 10 minutes   *Cooking Time: 30 minutes*   *Servings: 2*

Ingredients:

- 2 taco shells, warmed in the microwave for 10 seconds to make them fresh.
- For the Slaw:
- 1 cup red cabbage, shredded
- 1 cup green cabbage, shredded
- 2 scallions, chopped
- 1 cup carrots, sliced
- For the Dressing:
- 1 tbsp sriracha
- ¼ cup apple cider vinegar
- ¼ tsp salt
- 2 tbsp sesame oil
- 1 tbsp Dijon mustard
- 1 tbsp lime juice
- ½ tbsp tamari
- 1 tbsp maple syrup
- ¼ tsp salt

Directions:

1. First, make the dressing and whisk all the ingredients in a small bowl until mixed well.
2. Next, combine the slaw ingredients in another bowl. Add the dressing and toss well.
3. Finally, take a taco shell and place the slaw in it.
4. Serve and enjoy.

Nutrition Facts (per serving):
Calories: 305 kcal, Fats: 15.6 g, Carbs: 34.8 g, Proteins: 6.8 g

124. Roasted Asparagus

Preparation Time: 10 minutes   *Cooking Time: 15 minutes*   *Servings: 4*

Ingredients:

- 4 tbsp olive oil,
- 4 tbsp Pecorino romano cheese, grated
- 1 ½ lb (680 g) asparagus, trimmed
- ½ tsp cayenne pepper
- Salt
- Black pepper
- Sriracha sauce
- Fresh cilantro, for garnish

Directions:

1. Toss your asparagus with olive oil, cheese, cayenne pepper, salt, black pepper, and sriracha sauce; toss until well coated.
2. Place the asparagus on a roasting pan. Roast in the preheated oven at 420°F (216°C) for 10 minutes
3. Rotate the pan and cook for an additional 4 to 5 minutes. Serve immediately, garnished with fresh cilantro. Bon appétit!

Nutrition Facts (per serving):
Calories: 241 kcal, Fats: 18.5 g, Proteins: 10.6 g, Carbs: 7.7 g

125. Vegan Tofu Spinach Lasagna

Preparation Time: 15 minutes   *Cooking Time: 30 minutes*   *Servings: 3*

Ingredients:

- 10 oz lasagna noodles
- 20 oz bag of spinach, thawed
- 14 oz firm tofu
- 4 cups tomato sauce
- 1 tsp salt
- ¼ cup soy milk
- ½ tsp garlic powder
- 2 tbsp lime juice
- 3 tbsp basil, fresh and chopped

Directions:

1. First, place the tofu along with the soy milk, salt, garlic powder, basil, and lime juice into a high-speed blender.
2. Blend for 1 to 2 minutes or until smooth.
3. After that, stir in the spinach and mash well.
4. Now, pour the tomato sauce into the pot.
5. Then layer ⅓ of the lasagna noodles and then ⅓ of the spinach and tofu mixture on top of it. Repeat the layers until all ingredients are used up. Next, cook for 6 to 8 hours in the slow cooker.
6. Serve it hot.

Nutrition Facts (per serving):
Calories: 361 kcal, Fats: 9.1 g, Carbs: 44.9 g, Proteins: 25.2 g

126. Sesame Tofu With Soba Noodles

Preparation Time: 10 minutes   *Cooking Time: 15 minutes*   *Servings: 4*

Ingredients:

- 2 cups cabbage, shredded
- 1 lb Soba noodles
- 14 oz firm tofu, cubed
- 2 green onions, thinly sliced
- 2 tbsp soy sauce
- ¼ cup rice vinegar
- 1 garlic clove, crushed
- 1 tbsp sesame oil
- 2 green onions, thinly sliced
- Peanuts, crushed, for garnishing
- 1 tsp vegetable oil
- 1 tsp fresh ginger, grated
- 1 tsp sesame seeds
- Water

Directions:

1. Boil 4 cups of water in a large pot over medium heat.
2. Once it starts boiling, add the noodles.
3. Cook the noodles by following the manufacturer's instructions.
4. Wash the noodles under cold water and then drain. Keep it aside.
5. After that, mix rice vinegar, sesame seeds, soy sauce, and sesame oil in a small bowl until well combined.
6. Next, spoon the oil into a heated skillet over medium-high heat.
7. Once the oil becomes hot, stir in the tofu.
8. Cook them for 4 minutes or until browned. Set it aside.
9. Now, spoon in ginger, cabbage, and garlic into the skillet.
10. Sauté them for 2 minutes or until softened.
11. Finally, mix the noodles, rice wine mixture, cabbage, tofu, and green onions in a large mixing bowl. Toss well.
12. Serve after topping it with peanuts.
13. Tip; for a spicier kick, you can use sriracha sauce on the noodles.

Nutrition Facts (per serving):
Calories: 318 kcal, Fats: 9.8 g, Carbs: 43 g, Proteins: 14.4 g

127. Spaghetti Squash With Tempeh

Preparation Time: 10 minutes   *Cooking Time: 45 minutes*   *Servings: 5*

Ingredients:

- 2 tbsp tamari
- 1 tbsp canola oil
- 12 oz tempeh, cubed
- 25 oz pasta sauce
- ¼ cup mirin
- 2 ½ lb Squash, halved lengthwise and seeded
- 1 cup baby spinach
- 2 garlic cloves, finely chopped
- 2 cups broccoli florets

Directions:

1. Preheat the oven to 375°F.
2. After that, combine garlic, tempeh, and mirin in a medium-sized bowl.
3. Toss them well and allow the mixture to marinate for half an hour.
4. In the meantime, place the halved squash on a large baking sheet with the cut sides down.
5. Bake them for 35 to 40 minutes or until tender.
6. Once cooked, allow it to cool, and spoon out the insides with a fork to get the noodles separated.
7. Heat oil in a large-sized saucepan over medium heat.
8. Add the tempeh to the pan and cook for 8 minutes or until tender.
9. In the meantime, place the pasta sauce in a saucepan over medium heat.
10. Finally, stir the broccoli into the pasta sauce and cook for a further five minutes or until softened.
11. Place the spaghetti on the plate and top it with the tempeh and broccoli mixture.
12. Tip: instead of mirin, you can also use honey.

Nutrition Facts (per serving):
Calories: 248 kcal, Fats: 8.6 g, Carbs: 21.7 g, Proteins: 21.8 g

128. Spaghetti With Chickpeas Meatballs

Preparation Time: 10 minutes *Cooking Time: 35 minutes* *Servings: 4*

Ingredients:

- ½ cup breadcrumbs
- 1 tsp Italian seasoning
- ¼ cup flax seeds
- 14 oz can chickpeas, drained
- ½ tsp salt
- 2 tsp onion powder
- 8 tbsp water
- ½ tbsp garlic powder
- ¼ cup Nutritional yeast

For the Pasta:

- 1 lb Spaghetti
- 25 oz pasta sauce

Directions:

1. First, preheat the oven to 325°F. After that, combine the flax seeds with water in a small bowl and set them aside for 5 minutes.
2. Next, place the chickpeas and salt in the food processor and process them for one minute or until you get a smooth mixture.
3. Now, transfer the chickpea mixture and the flaxseed mixture to a large mixing bowl. Stir well. Once combined, add all the remaining ingredients to the bowl.
4. Give everything a good stir and mix well.
5. Then, make balls from this mixture and arrange them on a parchment paper-lined baking sheet while leaving ample space between them. Bake them for 30 to 35 minutes. Turn them once halfway through.
6. Add the pasta sauce to a saucepan and warm it on medium heat. Add the meatballs to the sauce and stir to combine.
7. In the meantime, cook the spaghetti al dente by following the instructions given in the packet.
8. Finally, place the spaghetti on the serving plate and top it with the meatballs and pasta sauce.
9. Serve and enjoy.

Nutrition Facts (per serving):
Calories: 460 kcal, Fats: 9 g, Carbs: 75 g, Proteins: 19.8 g

Preparation Time: 15 minutes   *Cooking Time: 20 minutes*   *Servings: 2*

Ingredients:

- 2 heads cauliflower, sliced lengthwise into 'steaks.'
- ¼ cup olive oil
- ¼ cup chili sauce
- 2 tsp Erythritol
- Salt and black pepper to taste
- 2 shallots, diced
- A bunch green beans trimmed
- Fresh lemon juice
- 1 cup water
- Dried parsley to garnish

Directions:

1. Mix the olive oil, chili sauce, and erythritol in a bowl or container.
2. Brush the cauliflower with the mixture. Grill for 6 minutes. Flip the cauliflower, and cook further for 6 minutes.
3. Let the water boil, place the green beans in a sieve, and set over the steam from the boiling water.
4. Cover with a clean napkin to keep the steam trapped in the sieve.
5. Cook for 6 minutes
6. After, remove to a bowl and toss with lemon juice.
7. Remove the grilled caulis to a plate, and sprinkle with salt, pepper, shallots, and parsley. Serve with steamed green beans.

Nutrition Facts (per serving):
Calories: 373 kcal, Fats: 30.4 g, Carbs: 12.1 g, Proteins: 12.8 g

130. Sweet & Sour Tempeh

Preparation Time: 10 minutes   *Cooking Time: 30 minutes*   *Servings: 4*

Ingredients:

- 10 oz tempeh cut into 15mm blocks
- 2 tbsp olive oil
- 2 tbsp oy sauce
- ¾ cup vegetable broth

For the Sauce:

- 1 tbsp cornstarch
- 15 oz pineapple chunks, drained and juice kept separate
- 1 yellow onion, chopped
- 1 cup mushrooms, sliced
- ¼ cup vinegar
- 1 red bell pepper, chopped

Directions:

1. To make this delightful fare, heat a large skillet over medium-high heat.
2. Place the tempeh along with the vegetable broth and soy sauce in it.
3. Braise the tempeh for about 8 to 10 minutes or until soft.
4. After that, remove the skillet from the heat, remove the tempeh, and keep the braising liquid.
5. Take another skillet and spoon olive oil into it.
6. Heat it over medium heat and stir in the braised tempeh.
7. Cook the tempeh for three minutes or until browned.
8. In the meantime, to make the sauce, combine the braising liquid, reserved pineapple juice, vinegar, and cornstarch in a saucepan.
9. Heat the saucepan over medium heat and bring the mixture to a simmer while stirring it continuously. Then, add the onion, mushrooms, and red pepper to it and continue stirring until the mixture thickens. Finally, lower the heat and stir in the braised tempeh and pineapple chunks, then simmer for another five minutes.
10. Serve it hot.

Nutrition Facts (per serving):
Calories: 295 kcal, Fats: 12.9 g, Carbs: 25.4 g, Proteins: 19.3 g

131. Vegan Sloppy Joes

Preparation Time: 10 minutes   *Cooking Time: 20 minutes*   *Servings: 4*

Ingredients:

- 1 ½ cup tomato sauce
- 1 tbsp extra virgin olive oil
- ⅛ tsp ground black pepper
- ⅛ tsp cayenne pepper
- 1 tsp sweet paprika
- 2 garlic cloves
- 2 tsp onion powder
- 1¼ onion, chopped
- 2 tsp garlic powder
- 1 red bell pepper, chopped
- 1 green bell pepper, chopped
- 2 tbsp tomato paste
- 15 oz lentils, cooked
- 2 tbsp oy sauce
- 6 whole wheat hamburger buns

Directions:

1. To start, heat a large skillet over medium-high heat. Spoon in the oil, and once the oil becomes hot, add the veggies and cayenne pepper—sauté for 6 minutes or until golden brown. Stir occasionally. Next, stir all the remaining ingredients except the buns into the skillet and cook them for ten to twelve minutes or until the mixture thickens.
2. Finally, cut the buns in half and fill them with the filling.
3. Serve and enjoy.

Nutrition Facts (per serving):
Calories: 544 kcal, Fats: 14.4 g, Carbs: 82.3 g, Proteins: 21.2 g

CHAPTER 14
Sweets Recipes

132. Baked Apples

Preparation Time: 10 minutes   *Cooking Time: 30 minutes*   *Servings: 4*

Ingredients:
- 4 apples, sliced
- ½ tsp cinnamon
- 1 tbsp olive oil

Directions:
1. Place the sliced apples with olive and cinnamon into the cooking pot.
2. Cover the instant pot with the lid.
3. Select bake mode and set the temperature to 375°F and time for 30 minutes.
4. Serve and enjoy.

Nutrition Facts (per serving):
Calories: 108 kcal, Fats: 4.2 g, Carbs: 17.2 g, Proteins: 0.3 g

133. Berry Yogurt

Preparation Time: 20 minutes   *Cooking Time: 0 minutes*   *Servings: 2*

Ingredients:
- 1 cup plain yogurt
- 1 tbsp lemon juice
- 4 cups blackberries

Directions:
1. Place all ingredients inside a blender.
2. Blend until smooth. Pour into a container and cover.
3. Place in the fridge to set for two hours before serving.

Nutrition Facts (per serving):
Calories: 169 kcal, Fats: 4.9 g, Carbs: 22.7 g, Proteins: 8.7 g

134. Bean Brownies

Preparation Time: 30 minutes   *Cooking Time: 55 minutes*   *Servings: 10*

Ingredients:

For the Bean Brownies:

- 20 soft dates (soaked in hot water for 10 minutes)
- 1 cup kidney beans (drained weight; can)
- ½ cup rapeseed oil
- ½ cup almond drink (almond milk) (or other vegetable milk)
- 3 eggs
- 1/3 cup delicate oat flakes
- ½ cup ground almond kernels
- ½ cup cocoa powder
- 1 tsp baking powder
- 1 pinch salt
- 5 tbsp chopped walnut kernels

For the Frosting:

- 1 ripe avocado
- 3 tbsp coconut oil (melted)
- 3 tbsp espresso
- 3 tbsp cocoa powder
- 5 tbsp maple syrup
- Streusel or coarse sea salt as desired

Directions:

1. Puree the dates and kidney beans in a blender, food processor, or with a hand blender to a creamy purée.
2. Add rapeseed oil, almond drink, eggs, oat flakes, ground almonds, cocoa powder, baking powder, and salt to the date and bean puree and stir to make a brownie batter.
3. Fold the chopped walnuts into the dough and pour the dough into a baking dish (approx. 26 x 20 centimeters) lined with baking paper. Bake in a preheated oven at 180°C for about 30 minutes. Then let it cool down completely.
4. Now process all the ingredients for the frosting with a hand blender or a food processor into a fine chocolate cream and use a spatula to spread over the bean brownie. Refine with toppings as desired, cut into 16 pieces, and store in the refrigerator.

Nutrition Facts (per serving):
Calories: 356 kcal, Fats: 24.2 g, Carbs: 26.9 g, Proteins: 7.7 g

135. Raspberry Sorbet

Preparation Time: 10 minutes   *Cooking Time: 0 minutes*   *Servings: 2*

Ingredients:
- 1 tbsp honey
- ¼ cup coconut water
- 12 oz raspberries

Directions:
1. Place all ingredients inside a blender.
2. Blend until it is nice and smooth.
3. Pour it into a container and add the lid. Add to the freezer to set for a few hours before serving.

Nutrition Facts (per serving):
Calories: 131 kcal, Fats: 3.8 g, Carbs: 7.9 g, Proteins: 3.3 g

136. Brownie Cheesecake

Preparation Time: 50 minutes   *Cooking Time: 30 minutes*   *Servings: 10*

Ingredients:
- 4 cups dark chocolate (70% cocoa content)
- 2 tsp olive oil
- 3 eggs
- 1 ¼ cup quark (20% fat)
- 1 cup spelled flour type 1050
- ½ packet baking powder
- ½ tsp Vanilla powder
- 1 pinch salt

Directions:
1. For the chocolate mass, roughly chop the chocolate over a hot, non-boiling water bath. Then let it cool down a little.
2. Stir in the eggs and quark. Mix the flour with baking powder, vanilla, and salt and stir the flour mixture into the olive oil. Divide the dough and stir in the chocolate under half.
3. Fill the baking tin alternately in 3–4 layers and carefully marble with a fork. Cut into pieces for serving.

Nutrition Facts (per serving):
Calories: 230 kcal, Fats: 17.2 g, Carbs: 11.9 g, Proteins: 6.7 g

137. Chocolate Pudding

Preparation Time: 20 minutes　　*Cooking Time: 0 minutes*　　*Servings: 10*

Ingredients:
- 1 cup almond milk
- 1 cup chocolate chips
- 2 chopped avocados
- 1 tbsp cocoa powder
- ¼ cup creamy almond butter
- 1 tsp vanilla essence

Directions:
1. Add the milk and chocolate chips to the microwave for ½ minute and stir. Continue until melted.
2. Add in the rest of the ingredients and stir until smooth.
3. Let it set in the fridge for half an hour before serving.

Nutrition Facts (per serving):
Calories: 239 kcal, Fats: 20.2 g, Carbs: 10.5 g, Proteins: 3.5 g

---

138. Zucchini Brownies

Preparation Time: 30 minutes　　*Cooking Time: 55 minutes*　　*Servings: 5*

Ingredients:
- 2 cups zucchini
- ¼ cup coconut oil
- ½ cup dark chocolate (70% cocoa content)
- ½ cup + 2 tbsp whole meal spelled flour
- ½ cup + 2 tbsp spelled flour (type 630)
- ½ cup cocoa powder
- 1 tsp baking powder
- ½ tsp Vanilla powder
- 1 pinch salt
- 2 eggs

Directions:
1. Wash and grate the zucchini. Put in a sieve and squeeze out some liquid. Melt coconut oil in a small saucepan over low heat. Roughly chop the chocolate.
2. Put flour, cocoa powder, baking powder, vanilla powder, salt, eggs, and liquid coconut oil in a bowl. Process all ingredients with the whisk of a hand mixer to smooth the dough. Mix in the zucchini well, and fold in the chocolate.
3. Pour the dough into a pan lined with baking paper and smooth it out. Then let it cool completely in the mold. Cut into pieces and enjoy.

Nutrition Facts (per serving):
Calories: 380 kcal, Fats: 21.3 g, Carbs: 35.4 g, Proteins: 11.5 g

139. Strawberry Bruschetta

Preparation Time: 15 minutes   *Cooking Time: 0 minutes*   *Servings: 10*

Ingredients:

- 1 loaf sliced Ciabatta bread
- 8 oz goat cheese
- 1 cup basil leaves
- 2 containers strawberries, sliced
- 5 tbsp balsamic glaze

Directions:

1. Wash and slice strawberries; set aside. Wash and chop the basil leaves; set aside. Slice the ciabatta bread and spread some goat cheese evenly on each slice; add strawberries, and balsamic glaze, then top with basil leaves.
2. Serve on a platter.

Nutrition Facts (per serving):
Calories: 113 kcal, Fats: 4 g, Carbs: 14.1 g, Proteins: 4.9 g

140. Cashew Pudding

Preparation Time: 10 minutes   *Cooking Time: 25 minutes*   *Servings: 8*

Ingredients:

- ¼ cup cocoa powder, unsweetened
- 1 cup cashews, raw
- a dash of sea salt
- 4 tbsp almond milk, unsweetened
- 2 medjool dates
- 1 tbsp maple syrup
- 1 tbsp coconut oil

Directions:

1. First, place the cashews in a medium bowl along with hot water. Soak it for one hour.
2. Next, transfer the soaked cashews into a high-speed blender along with the remaining ingredients.
3. Blend for 2 minutes or until you get a smooth and creamy mixture.
4. Now, return the pudding to the bowl and cover it with plastic wrap.
5. Finally, keep the bowl in the refrigerator for 2 to 3 hours or until set.
6. Serve and enjoy.

Nutrition Facts (per serving):
Calories: 158 kcal, Proteins: 4.6 g, Carbs: 10 g, Fats: 11.1 g

141. Vanilla Mug Cake

🌿 Preparation Time: 1 minutes   *🍲 Cooking Time: 4 minutes*   *🍽 Servings: 1*

Ingredients:

- ¼ cup cashew milk
- 1 scoop vanilla protein powder
- ¼ tsp vanilla extract
- 1 tsp chocolate chips
- ½ tsp baking powder
- 1 tbsp granulated sweetener of your choice
- 1 tbsp coconut flour

Directions:

1. Start by applying baking spray all over a microwave-safe mug.
2. To this, stir in the protein powder, coconut flour, baking powder, and granulated sweetener. Mix well.
3. Now, pour the cashew milk into the flour mixture along with the vanilla extract. If the combination seems crumbly, add more milk until you get a thick batter.
4. Next, cook in the microwave for 1 minute or until the center is set and cooked.
5. Serve and enjoy.

Nutrition Facts (per serving):
Calories: 199 kcal, Proteins: 15.5 g, Carbs: 8.1 g, Fats: 13.3 g

142. Raspberry Nuts Parfait

🌿 Preparation Time: 15 minutes   *🍲 Cooking Time: 10 minutes*   *🍽 Servings: 1*

Ingredients:

- ¼ cup frozen raspberries
- ¼ cup frozen blueberries
- ¼ cup toasted, thinly sliced almonds
- 1 cup nonfat plain Greek yogurt
- 2 tsp raw honey

Directions:

1. First, layer Greek yogurt in a parfait glass; add berries; layer yogurt again, top with almonds and more berries; drizzle with honey.
2. Serve chilled.

Nutrition Facts (per serving):
Calories: 386 kcal, Fats: 22.7 g, Carbs: 29.8 g, Proteins: 16 g

CHAPTER 15
Conversion Tables

TEMPERATURES EQUIVALENTS	
FAHRENHEIT (°F)	**CELSIUS (°C)**
225	107
250	120
275	135
300	150
325	160
350	180
375	190
400	205
425	220
450	235
475	245
500	260

WEIGHT EQUIVALENTS

US STANDARD	METRIC (g)
1 oz	28
2 oz	57
5 oz	142
10 oz	284
15 oz	425
16 oz (1 pound)	455
1.5 pounds	680
2 pounds	907

VOLUME EQUIVALENTS (LIQUID)

US STANDARD	US STANDARD (OUNCES)	METRIC (APPROXIMATE)
1 teaspoon	0.17 fl.oz.	5 mL
1 tablespoon	0.5 fl.oz.	15 mL
2 tablespoons	1 fl.oz.	30 mL
1/4 cup	2 fl.oz	60 mL
1/2 cup	4 fl.oz	120 mL
1 cup	8 fl.oz	240 mL
1 1/2 cup	12 fl.oz	355 mL
2 cups or 1 pint	16 fl.oz	475 mL
4 cups or 1 quart	33 fl.oz	0.95 L
1 gallon	128 fl.oz	3.78 L

US STANDARD			METRIC (APPROXIMATE)
3 teaspoons	1 tablespoon	1/2 ounce	14 g
2 tablespoons	1/8 cup	1 ounce	28 g
4 tablespoons	1/4 cup	2 ounces	57 g
8 tablespoons	1/2 cup	4 ounces	114 g
12 tablespoons	3/4 cup	6 ounces	170 g
16 tablespoons	1 cup	8 ounces	227 g
32 tablespoons	2 cups	16 ounces (1 pound)	455 g

VOLUME EQUIVALENTS (SOLID)

US STANDARD	METRIC (APPROXIMATE)
1/8 teaspoon	0.5 mL
1/4 teaspoon	1 mL
1/2 teaspoon	2 mL
3/4 teaspoon	4 mL
1 teaspoon	5 mL
1 tablespoon	15 mL
1/4 cup	59 mL
1/2 cup	118 mL
3/4 cup	177 mL
1 cup	235 mL
2 cups	475 mL

Conclusion

Thank you for reading this cookbook. Weight loss surgery, whether surgery or with a gastric band, effectively reduces your stomach's capacity. It reduces the volume to the size of a small egg. A smaller stomach restricts the amount of food you can eat, resulting in a lower calorie intake and, as a result, weight loss. The diet helps your body gradually learn to tolerate and appreciate nutritious meals at a healthy pace after weight loss surgery. Your new weight loss surgical diet encourages healthy eating and portion control with meals high in protein and low in fat. These newly discovered methods of eating a nutritious diet after weight loss surgery will help encourage and sustain your weight loss over time as your stomach stretches as you recover.

It makes no difference which method of bariatric surgery you choose; it is a life-changing procedure. To succeed, you must change your perspective on life and food choices. This may be more difficult than the actual surgery and recovery process. Here's how you'll have to change your perspective.

You must first prepare those around you before you get to your mindset. Consider including those closest to you in the process. This will help them understand what is going on and how they can best assist you. Of course, you won't have to share your decision to have bariatric surgery with people who aren't in your inner circle or who may only have negative things to say about it. Surgery is a personal decision, and I recommend that you only discuss it with people you know will support and encourage you. Don't be discouraged if someone you thought would be understanding turns out to be against it. It's usually because they don't understand the process or they're afraid of what might happen.

Remind yourself that the only person you have to answer to is yourself. Keep your head held high and amaze those who doubt you with an amazing transformation!

Best wishes!

Alphabetical Index

P

R

S

T

References

Faria SL, O'Kane M. The importance of a cookbook for patients who have bariatric surgery. In Nutrition and Bariatric Surgery 2021 Jan 1 (pp. 257-282). Academic Press.

Puzziferri N, Roshek TB, Mayo HG, Gallagher R, Belle SH, Livingston EH. Long-term follow-up after bariatric surgery: a systematic review. Jama. 2014 Sep 3312(9):934-42.

Faria GF, Santos JM, Simonson Dcup Quality of life after gastric sleeve and gastric bypass for morbid obesity. Porto biomedijournal. 2017 Mar 12(2):40-6.

Coleman KJ, Fischer H, Arterburn DE, Barthold D, Barton LJ, Basu A, Courcoulas A, Crawford CL, Fedorka P, Kim B, Mun E. Effectiveness of gastric bypass versus gastric sleeve for cardiovascular disease: protocol and baseline results for a comparative effectiveness study. JMIR Research Protocols. 2020 Apr 69(4):e14936.

Printed in Great Britain
by Amazon

29208495R00071